BARNEY

Also by Michael Rosenthal

Virginia Woolf

*The Character Factory: Baden-Powell's Boy Scouts and the
Imperatives of Empire*

*Nicholas Miraculous: The Amazing Career of the Redoubtable
Dr. Nicholas Murray Butler*

BARNEY

Grove Press and Barney Rosset

America's Maverick Publisher and His Battle against Censorship

MICHAEL ROSENTHAL

Arcade Publishing • New York

First Edition

Unless otherwise credited, the photographs in the photo insert are reprinted by the kind permission of Astrid Myers Rosset and the Barney Rosset estate.

Arcade Publishing books may be purchased in bulk at special discounts for sales promotion, corporate gifts, fund-raising, or educational purposes. Special editions can also be created to specifications. For details, contact the Special Sales Department, Arcade Publishing, 307 West 36th Street, 11th Floor, New York, NY 10018 or arcade@skyhorsepublishing.com.

Arcade Publishing® is a registered trademark of Skyhorse Publishing, Inc.®, a Delaware corporation.

Visit our website at www.arcadepub.com.

10 9 8 7 6 5 4 3 2 1

Library of Congress Cataloging-in-Publication Data is available on file.
Library of Congress Cataloging in Publication Control Number: 2016052307

Cover design by Erin Seaward-Hiatt
Front cover photograph by Bob Adelman, courtesy Bob Adelman Books, Inc.

ISBN: 978-1-62872-650-3
Ebook ISBN: 978-1-62872-652-7

Printed in the United States of America

For the newest generation:

Eli, Ian, Matthew, Thea

"This cheap, exploitative, radical, avant-garde, courageous, daring, pandering, freedom-loving, woman-debasing, stupid, trashy, noble, tight-fisted, profligate press managed, almost always, to provoke or charm some group or other."

—Gilbert Sorrentino

"We are still reaping the fruits of your relentless efforts and achievements, and such is your legacy that the American public is indebted to you for many of the most interesting books it reads."

—French Minister of Culture in designating Rosset Commandeur de l'Ordre des Arts et Lettres

"To Barney Rosset, for distinctive and continuous service to international letters, to the freedom and dignity of writers, and to the free transmission of the printed word across the barriers of poverty, ignorance censorship and repression."

—PEN American Center, Ninth Publisher Citation, 1988

"Was Grove controversial? The word is too pale for the tempests at Grove, whether lawsuits, death-threats, grenade attacks by Cubans or occupation of the premises by enraged feminists. Say rather that it was a valve for pressurized cultural energies, a breach in the dam of American Puritanism—a whiplashing live cable of Zeitgeist."

—Barney Rosset's own description of Grove Press

CONTENTS

BARNEY

INTRODUCTION

Before Barney Rosset, no book publisher in American history had his office blown up because his political views were found offensive. Enraged at Rosset's support of Fidel Castro and Che Guevara, nine Cuban anti-Castro reserve officers in the American Air Force changed that in the summer of 1968. The rocket-propelled grenade they fired into the second-floor window of Grove Press from a pickup truck eloquently testified to Rosset's capacity to provoke American sensibilities. A self-delighting maverick, an impetuous outsider who took enormous pleasure in confronting American conformity and prudery, Barney Rosset was unquestionably the most daring and arguably the most significant American book publisher of the twentieth century. Quick to rush in where respectable publishers feared to tread, he brought to the reading public the European avant-garde, radical political and literary voices, steamy Victorian erotica, and banned writers such as D. H. Lawrence, Henry Miller, and William Burroughs.

Blending the countercultural and New Left with the mainstream through Grove Press and the magazine—*Evergreen Review*—it subsequently launched, he both helped create and inserted himself firmly into the center of the cultural ferment of the sixties. Whatever was contentious and relevant in this tempestuous decade—sexual, political, racial—there were Barney and his books. Grove Press provided the intellectual fuel for the revolutionary energies coursing through colleges and universities. It delivered a leftist message of liberation from the old and the outworn—along with a reading list of exciting new authors. No serious student's bookshelves could be considered complete without displaying a substantial array of Grove paperbacks.

Barney's landmark legal battles against the stultifying censorship laws changed forever the nature of writing and publishing in America. More than any other individual, he was responsible for freeing American literature from the shackles imposed by the conscientious watchdogs of morality. "It is hard to remember," Martin Garbus, the distinguished First Amendment lawyer, points out, "how puritanical America is and was. Barney was the guy who fundamentally broke down the censorship barriers in this country." He spent nearly $100,000 ($800,000 in today's dollars) during his two-year struggle (1959–60) with the powerful US Post Office to permit D. H. Lawrence's *Lady Chatterley's Lover* to be read in an unexpurgated version here. Had he lost, he might have been sentenced to jail for attempting to send forbidden materials through the mails. It took five years and roughly $250,000 (nearly $2,000,000 today), pushing Grove to the brink of bankruptcy, to earn the right for Henry Miller's *Tropic of Cancer* to be published in the United States. In order to convince booksellers to carry the book, in violation of local anti-obscenity ordinances, Barney elected to indemnify them for any court expenses incurred in answering charges about selling prohibited volumes. He funded sixty cases in twenty-one states before he finally won in the Supreme Court in 1964.

Two years later, in 1966, he got a Massachusetts appellate court to agree, despite one judge's characterization of it as "a revolting miasma of unrelieved perversion," that William Burroughs's *Naked Lunch* was serious literature, entitled to constitutional protection. The decision, according to novelist Norman Mailer, "changed the literary history of America. It opened up the possibilities. After that, American publishers were pretty much willing to print anything."

A man with a joyous, fully fleshed sense of his own importance, he believed his mission as a publisher was to serve as "protector and guardian" of the creative spirit, dedicated to opposing anything that might restrict the liberty of writers. Wallace Fowlie, Barney's professor of French literature at The New School, praised his tenacity in pursuit of his ideals: "He fights for good causes, and he fights hard. He would have made a first-rate crusader under St. Louis. In fact," he added after further consideration, "he would have made a good St. Louis in the thirteenth century." Barney's commitment to total freedom of expression—"I feel personally there hasn't been a word written or uttered that shouldn't be published"—essentially demarcates the before and after of American publishing. In defending the right of words of every kind to be read, he made Grove a place for the high and the low, Nobel Prize-winners and authors of nineteenth-century spanking novels. He admired them both—his Nobelists, Samuel Beckett, Pablo Neruda, Octavio Paz, Kenzaburo Oe, Mario Vargas-Llosa, Harold Pinter—and his mostly anonymous pornographers. Because the dirty books in his Victorian paperback library sold well, people frequently assume Barney published them simply for money. But that is to misunderstand Barney. He liked sex. He liked to engage in it, with a multitude of girlfriends, call girls, and a variety of wives. He liked to read about it. He thought there was nothing wrong with being turned on by a book. Barney's erotica might have been profitable, but he also found it pleasurable. One of his favorite books was *The Story of O*, the enormously popular French novel of female submission that Grove brought out in English translation in 1965.

He must have felt it a gratifying irony that the "Old Smut Peddler," as he was known by some in the 1960s, who spent his career being derided by the publishing establishment because of his affection for things pornographic, hard- as well as soft-core, should have received, in 2008, a Lifetime Achievement Award from the National Book Foundation honoring his "vision and enormous contributions to American publishing."

The acquisition of a more or less defunct press with an inventory of three little-known paperback volumes would hardly seem the most direct path to earning a Lifetime Achievement Award from the book industry. It is safe to say that when Barney, in 1951, followed the suggestion of a soon-to-be ex-wife and purchased Grove Press for $3,000 from its two dysfunctional partners, even he had no idea what extraordinary consequences would follow for American literary and political culture. A failed marriage, unrealized fantasies about becoming a writer, and a single, flawed effort as a documentary filmmaker are not generally accepted predictors of success in the publishing world. Barney had neither business credentials nor a record of accomplishment when he stumbled into publishing. Instead, he possessed what one admirer called "a whim of steel," extraordinary courage, a kind of instinctive genius that encouraged him to take chances, and a ferocious competitiveness. Together, they served him well in his understanding of the role of publishers as "in effect the foot-soldiers in the struggle against hypocrisy and oppression."

If he saw himself as a humble foot soldier, it is clear that he simultaneously functioned as commander in chief in the battle. No other publisher embraced the risks he did; no other publisher exercised a comparable influence on the cultural landscape of this country. He conducted his campaign against censorship the same way he lived his personal life, by adhering to a simple rule: "My first impulse is always, 'Do it.'" In obeying its strictures, he partied a lot (with the Beats and Norman

5

Mailer); drank a lot (with the painters Willem de Kooning, Jackson Pollock, and Franz Kline, among others) at the Cedar Bar in Greenwich Village and elsewhere; bought Robert Motherwell's house in East Hampton; took (once) LSD that Timothy Leary himself gave him; and married five wives, four of whom left him. He made and lost money doing exactly what pleased him: "All my life I followed the things that I liked— people, things, books—and when things were offered me I published them. I never did anything I didn't like."

Doing only what he liked made Grove a special kind of company and Barney a unique boss. He just didn't care about what other publishers were concerned with: sales figures, cost projections, audiences, editorial meetings. He wanted to build a company publishing books he valued and enjoyed, surrounded by interesting people who shared his vision. He succeeded brilliantly. Grove was different because Barney was different. In place of a smoothly operating organization, there was drama and chaos, mostly created by Barney, who loved thrills. "The Auntie Mame of publishing," one of his editors called him. "Grove is not average," Barney insisted, "it's a weird aberration." He gloried in his maverick status, going his own blue-jeaned, turtle-necked, idiosyncratic way. When informed by an admirer that he was seen as the Clint Eastwood of the business, Barney admitted he rather liked the notion. He took the accusation of Robert Bernstein, president of Random House, that he stood "outside the mainstream of American publishing" as a compliment. Kenzaburo Oe, the Nobel Prize–winning Japanese novelist who became Barney's dear friend, thought of him as Huckleberry Finn.

Barney relished the merging of his work and his life. He thought of Grove Press as an extension of his personality. Barney at work and Barney at play were inseparable. "My private life," he declared, "sometimes mirrored the fiction I published." When in 1962 he issued Robert Gover's *One Hundred Dollar Misunderstanding*, whose protagonist is a charming, beautiful black call girl, he selected for the cover a photograph of the charming, beautiful black call girl he was currently seeing.

Barney lived both his professional and personal life at warp speed. Editor Fred Jordan observed that Barney "always seemed to be on the run, even when he was sitting down." Eating and sleeping were minor afterthoughts for an existence sustained by gobbling amphetamines from a silver pillbox—a family heirloom he carried with him—and consuming vast amounts of alcohol: red wine in the morning, martinis at lunch, rum and cokes throughout the rest of the day and night. And night was for going out, with or without the wife of the moment. Rules and conventions—of publishing or human relations—were not for Barney. It's what made a job at Grove so exhilarating. And at the same time, somewhat precarious. Barney fired people with the same insouciance as he hired them—or hired them back. Herman Graf, vice president and sales director, recalls that Barney fired him twice and hired him three times. At the second firing, Barney assured him it had nothing to do with his work, which was satisfactory. It was "purely personal." Graf was puzzled but continued to think of him as his best boss ever. Claudia Menza, who worked her way up from editorial assistant on *Evergreen Review* to managing editor of

Grove, was fired once a year by Barney, and once a year she quit. Each time she simply showed up at work the next day and they both went on as if nothing had happened. But she remembers one day when Barney asked her to have lunch—a bad sign. Over lunch Barney told her, "This company isn't big enough for both of us. One of us has to go." She retorted, "I don't suppose that would be you." "No," he said, laughing, "it's been a good marriage, but now it's time for a divorce." However, they remained friends for the rest of Barney's life.

Almost no one who worked there can ever remember having had a better time. On the occasion that Grove employees received job offers with bigger salaries from larger publishing houses, Dick Seaver, his friend and associate commented, the response was inevitably the same: "We're having too much fun here." Barney happily listened to the book suggestions of the editors he brought to the company—Don Allen, Dick Seaver, Fred Jordan—whose enthusiasms for particular manuscripts were invariably enough for Barney. But the final decision always rested with him. Barney in the end published what Barney liked. And nothing else. Jordan emphasized that "he never really read with an audience in mind; he had himself in mind. . . . Barney basically just pleased himself and said so."

Running a business according to the tastes of its owner is not necessarily the best model for long-term fiscal stability. The practice succeeded in endowing the press with a unique personality and cultural identity, but it also left it vulnerable to the flaws in Barney's highly personal judgments. He didn't like Lawrence Durrell's *Justine*, for example, the first volume of his successful Alexandria Quartet, and summarily rejected it when it was offered to him in England. He didn't understand what Tolkien was all about and concluded no one else would either. He later realized he should have given it to his children to evaluate. And when he had the opportunity to publish what became a huge bestseller, Alex Comfort's *The Joy of Sex*, he turned it down because he found it too healthy and antiseptic for Grove's image. Sex, for Barney, was never intended to be so jolly.

Barney treasured especially those subversive writers who challenged and irritated, who pushed against the conventional, people like Kerouac and Ginsberg; John Rechy and Hubert Selby; Henry Miller and William Burroughs; Alain Robbe-Grillet, Eugène Ionesco, and Jean Genet; Samuel Beckett and David Mamet, Harold Pinter and Bertolt Brecht. In taking forbidden, offensive, and little-known work and finding an audience for it, Barney bestowed gifts on writers and readers everywhere.

John Rechy, whose harrowing novel of the gay underworld, *City of Night*, Rosset turned into a bestseller in 1963, emphasizes the debt a literate America owes Barney:

"Posterity repeatedly wins out over Sunday book reviewers, and many of the books excoriated when they were first published by Grove Press have left their detractors far, far behind and have become modern classics. Every publisher in the country, and every writer, gained from Barney Rosset's courage in battling censorship. When the prejudices about Grove Press fade, Barney Rosset will be given his due as one of the heroic figures in the arts in his time, and the 'Grove Press Years' will come to be recognized as high-water marks in American literature."

1
PRIVILEGED BEGINNINGS

Barney was born in Chicago in 1922, the sole child of a worka-
holic, successful Russian-Jewish banker and his Irish-Catholic
wife. His concern for social justice, his love of the subversive
and lifelong need to confront the establishment with its hypoc-
risies were not passions he inherited from his parents. They
harbored no such unsettling impulses. Barnet Lee Rosset Sr.
embraced all the conservative values Barney hated. Senior and
Junior had little in common besides their shared name. Barney
felt trapped between resenting him and being dependent on
him for strength and material support. He remembers his father
tearing up a biography of Lenin that a teacher had given him at
the progressive school to which his parents unaccountably sent
him in seventh grade. Except for some shady business associates, like the notorious gangster Meyer Lansky, with whom he

jointly owned the Hotel Nacional in Cuba, most of Senior's best friends consisted of Catholic priests, accounting for the peculiar fact that he is buried in a Catholic cemetery. Barney's beautiful mother, Mary Tansey, had no particular interests in priests, her husband's career, or her son's leftist politics. She preferred to drink and go to the horse races, frequently accompanied—in secret—by Barney, as Senior did not approve of Junior going to the track. "My mother was hooked on horses," Barney once observed, "and my father on priests." Although she always denied it, Barney insisted, to her face, that she was anti-Semitic.

While the freckled, stunning redhead represented a great catch for the Russian Jew, their marriage was abysmal. After Barnet Senior recovered from a bleeding ulcer in the 1930s, he joined Mary in turning into an alcoholic. Alfred Adler, a cousin of the famous psychoanalyst of the same name, who was one of Barney's high school teachers and became a kind of mentor to him, reports seeing husband and wife sitting at opposite ends of the large dining room table, in their Lake Shore Drive apartment, a bottle of gin in front of each of them. When, as an adult, Barney had to speak to his father over the phone, he always hoped Senior wouldn't come to the conversation drunk. The roots of Barney's own prodigious drinking are not hard to trace.

But whether drunk or not, Barnet Senior had a vexed relationship with his son, for he was unable to accommodate himself to Barney's contempt for the Rosset wealth. The pleasure Barney took in what Senior's money could buy—a horse, a car, vacation trips, an elegant apartment—never extended to his affirming the unjust social system of which he was a conspicuous beneficiary. Barney would later, only half-jokingly, describe himself as a Communist-Capitalist. A 1943 report on Barney by FBI special agent Nunzio Giabalvo, in addition to pointing out that he was left-handed, notes that "subject's father was very disturbed by subject's radical thoughts and activities and sternly opposed them. Subject's father is a wealthy banker in Chicago and is very much a capitalist. In fact, subject's actions in this regard have nearly broken his father's heart."

The cosseted existence of material pleasures was not without its accompanying demons. Barney remembers a profoundly disturbing dream as a little boy in which "I had an out-of-body experience, seeing myself as an object rocketing into space, zooming through a black void until I was transformed into a 'knob of blackness.' I knew I was experiencing the terror of my own death." For the rest of his life Barney, "hounded by that dream," could not sleep in a totally darkened room. Seventeen years of psychoanalysis still didn't permit him to turn the lights off.

Had Barnet Senior been more self-reflective, he would never have forgiven himself for sending Barney to the two progressive schools that nurtured his radical beliefs: the Gateway School and Francis W. Parker. With tiny classes of ten students or so and a relaxed, permissive ethos, Gateway was bad enough, but Parker, to which Barney went in the middle of the seventh grade when Gateway went bankrupt, was considerably worse. For Barney, there couldn't have been a more life-enhancing choice, even though a left-wing disaster for his father. "I was mad for it. It was my whole life. . . . I couldn't wait to get to school in the morning," Barney emphasized in a 1968 interview. He loved his five and one-half years there, claiming that nothing critical about him had changed since his graduation in 1940. Founded in 1901 by Colonel Parker, whom John Dewey called "the father of progressive education," it maintained that learning should be fun, an aid to the full and relaxed flourishing of the individual. Its motto—"everything to help and nothing to hinder"—perfectly suited Barney's needs and temperament. Work was never onerous; grades were not assigned on the basis of objective achievement but were rather tied to an assessment of individual capacity.

If the teachers were not actual card-carrying communists, they were at the very least well to the left of anything that Barnet Senior ever imagined. They supported the Republican side in the Spanish Civil War, the American labor movement, and the need to keep America out of any European conflict. Every year the students organized a strike for peace, with appropriately impassioned lectures offered by the faculty. When "Gone with the Wind" opened in Chicago in 1939, Barney picketed to protest its demeaning stereotypes of the blacks.

The classes served up a more or less steady diet of liberal ideas. Sarah Greenebaum, a beloved English teacher, taught Defoe's *Robinson Crusoe* to Barney's eighth-grade class by handing out her own mimeographed version in which the natives of the island organize to expel Crusoe for being a greedy capitalist intent on extorting money from them. The Parker parents didn't appreciate this recasting of Defoe's novel into a socialist tract, but Greenebaum didn't change the text to please them. Provoked by Jim Mitchell, a slightly alcoholic English teacher, to do something about their revolutionary ideals besides discussing them, Barney and two of his classmates decided, one evening in their sophomore year in 1938, to take over the school. Climbing to the top of the building, they planted a red flag of revolution (resembling a pirate flag more than anything else), declaring Parker to be a new country. Not all the students shared Barney's political fervor, however, and not all delighted in the takeover. One of Barney's good friends, Stuyvessant Van Buren, whose name clearly suggests closer ties to the DAR than to Moscow, was particularly opposed. The next morning, he ascended to the building's tower, still flying the red flag, with one of his family's handguns. Barney blanched when he saw the revolver, assured him it was all a joke, and promptly proclaimed the end of the revolution. It being the Parker School, nothing happened to the perpetrators.

Parker's laid-back, politically liberal atmosphere allowed Barney to do what he wanted to do, read the authors he wanted to read—John Steinbeck, James T. Farrell, Nelson Algren, Frank Norris—and stimulated him to continue to question American values. According to the indefatigable Nunzio Giabalvo, Parker caused Barney to entertain "thoughts that there should not be any rich men in the world." Such thoughts undoubtedly led him and his good friend Haskell Wexler, who went on to become a distinguished filmmaker, to join the American Student Union, a left-wing organization intended primarily for college students. Only in the eighth grade at Parker when they became members, they traveled by bus to Vassar for an ASU conference, not in the least troubled that they were years younger than everybody else.

Parker's influence on Barney's adult crusade against all forms of oppression and censorship is evident in a tenth-grade English paper he wrote, lamenting the failure of Americans to live up to the courage of their immigrant ancestors by taking their freedoms for granted. Young Barney's "True American" must "fight for freedom of the press and religious toleration. . . . They must vote for the best political candidates, regardless of party or anything else. Their ideas must always be progressive ones. They cannot be whining reactionaries. Today's American carries many responsibilities. He lives in the freest country on earth and he should keep it that way."

Barney rapidly became a star at Parker, in part because of his compulsion to challenge all limits. "Barney always wanted to see how much he could push himself," Wexler pointed out. "How far he could run until he was exhausted; how long he could hold his breath; how much booze he could drink before he passed out." Chosen co-captain of the football team (along with Wexler), Barney also distinguished himself as a track champion, holder of the Chicago private school record in the half-mile. He served as editor of the school paper, was elected senior class president, and remained always an outspoken critic of politics and mores he disliked. When Sarah Greenebaum encouraged students to put out mimeographed newsletters about their interests, he and Haskell coedited in eighth grade the "Sommunist" (a blending of socialism and communism), which contained a variety of left-wing sentiments and observations about the world, as well as some dirty jokes, that Greenebaum shortly terminated. The blatant political nature of the title generated some anxiety among school officials and parents; in response, the two editors decided to change it to the less provocative (but more revealing) "Anti-Everything," making it a kind of puerile precursor to the mature Barney's Grove Press. The experimental French novelist Alain Robbe-Grillet, whom Grove published, said in a 1983 interview, that Barney was "fascinated by everything that was against the established order, in whatever sense or direction it took. . . . He could get interested in anything . . . as long as it was anti-establishment."

Some of the heroic anti-establishment figures of the thirties whom Barney found intriguing were the fabled gangsters of the time—Al Capone, Machine Gun Kelly, Baby Face Nelson, and Bugsy Siegel, to name a few. Of these, Barney liked the bank robber John Dillinger the most, arguing that his initiative and skill were precisely what this country needed to pull itself out of the depression. While still at the Gateway School he wrote a letter to the government, recommending that Dillinger be protected, not prosecuted. He also, when applying to Parker, named Mussolini as the most important person in the modern world. This judgment, a result of having read George Seldes's *Sawdust Caesar*, a biography of the Italian dictator, later got distorted in official reports on Barney into the rather more incendiary assertion that Mussolini was the living man he most esteemed; it dogged Barney throughout the rest of his life. No subsequent investigation of his character, whether undertaken by the army, the FBI, or the CIA, failed to note his admiration for the fascist leader as proof of Barney's questionable loyalty to American values. And no one seemed interested in the fact that even had he celebrated Mussolini in this way (which he clearly did not), he did so when he was twelve.

In addition to shaping Barney's moral sensibilities and providing him an opportunity for athletic success, Parker introduced him to two women—girls at this point—who occupied his imagination for the rest of his life: Nancy Ashenhurst and Joan Mitchell. Joan, two years behind Barney at school, became his first wife (in 1949), but it was Nancy, a classmate, whom he initially adored. Barney thought her the most beautiful girl in the school. A seductive blonde, she was sought after by all the Parker boys but particularly by Haskell and Barney, who were always vying with each other for her affections, which she doled out with sufficient care to keep both interested. Although not athletic, a quality Barney liked in his women—Joan for example, excelled as a competitive figure skater—and lacking his political concerns, Nancy otherwise possessed all conceivable female virtues for Barney. She loved the theater, both as an actor and sophisticated director beyond her years, and was responsible for all the best undergraduate productions at Parker. Barney claimed his interest in theater—Grove would go on to corner the market on the twentieth-century's outstanding playwrights—Samuel Beckett, Jean Genet, Eugène Ionesco, Harold Pinter, Tom Stoppard, David Mamet—developed out of his attachment to

Nancy. Had she been absorbed in mathematics, he later quipped, he might well have become some form of mathematician.

Not everyone admired Nancy—Joan thought her "a pretentious jerk"—but Barney remained smitten. At fifteen, however, his bumbling inexperience made it difficult for him to know how to arrange the consummation of his desires for her. Here Parker's commitment never to hinder, only to help, played a decisive role. Barney had confided his despair to his admiring teacher and friend, Alfred Adler, called by Wexler "the school's unofficial meddler in psychological affairs," who determined that intervention was necessary. He spoke to Nancy's parents about his concern for Barney's well-being, urging them to understand his plight and make Nancy accessible to him. Alarmed at the thought of adolescent unhappiness and buying into the full Parker ethos of helpfulness, the parents shortly went off for the weekend, leaving both door and bed open to Nancy and her imagination. She informed Barney that her parents were gone and the apartment available, at which point, without any further assistance from dedicated faculty, he managed to take care of business on his own.

The triangular relationship between Nancy and her two suitors continued throughout their time at Parker, with Nancy favoring first one, then the other. At one point during their senior year, Haskell graciously renounced his interest in Nancy, ceding her to Barney. According to Barney, Haskell said, "'You know, I don't want Nancy anymore. You can have her.' And I said, 'Do you really mean that Haskell?' He said, 'Yes, I literally do.' I said, 'Thank you very, very much.' I meant it. I went to the phone and called her and said, 'Nancy, you're now mine again.'" Despite Haskell's gifting of Nancy to him, the stops and starts of the relationship between Barney and Nancy continued until March of 1941, when the two agreed to end it permanently. Barney was crushed—the thought that he might not see her again struck him "like a punch in the guts"—but he realized there was nothing to be done about it. He would dream about her for the rest of his life and regret the loss of what he cherished for a time as "the only thing in my life that meant anything." After Haskell called him in 1943 to announce his marriage to Nancy, Barney was both incredulous and despondent. "He married her, I was convinced, because I liked her. And he told other people that too, that I should have married her, not him."

Even with the turmoil surrounding Nancy, Barney always looked tenderly at his Parker years, producing in him a condition that he described as "life-long nostalgia" for the experience. Respected by his peers—his graduation yearbook describes him as "one of those unusual personalities who is outstanding in many fields, as a champion runner and in the classroom, where he has been a great asset by dint of his bountiful factual knowledge and definite ideas on almost every social issue"—he was admired by the faculty as well. Barney remained sensitive throughout his professional life to what he considered the low-grade anti-Semitism of the publishing world, and it must have come as a shock when he discovered that his own beloved Parker was not entirely free from it. Writing his official college recommendation, the school's principal, Herbert W. Smith, endorsed him in the highest terms, noting that "in spite of the depth of his emotions, and the fact that he has Jewish blood, he never obtrudes himself or his own ways on his comrades, and has none of the self-centered preoccupation with his own point of view that marks boys of Jewish extraction." Smith's exculpatory anti-Semitism aside, there could hardly be a more off-target assessment. Barney's manifold virtues did not include lack of self-absorption, and Grove Press stands as a stunning testament to the power of one man's point of view. Narcissism, perhaps more than any other trait, constituted Barney's defining characteristic. However misguided Smith's evaluation, his enthusiastic support of Barney guaranteed he would be admitted to the college of his choice. The only nagging question: which one? Barney expressed interest in two, Dartmouth and Swarthmore, and received acceptances from both. He knew very little about either, entertaining thoughts about Dartmouth more to placate his father than anything else, who rejoiced at the notion of a happily conservative school blessedly free from the pinko ideas and teachers that made Parker such a nightmare for him. With his whim of steel already well developed, Barney applied to Swarthmore for two appropriately capricious reasons. First, he liked the recruiter who came to Parker, claiming to have been an ambulance driver in the Spanish Civil War. As a young man, Barney was infatuated with the drama and idealism of the war, lamenting that he had been unable to participate. Discovering a connection to the action he had missed through the person of Swarthmore's representative weighed heavily in the school's favor. Second, and more important, Nancy was going to Vassar and Barney thought—incorrectly—that Swarthmore was nearby.

So without much, or even any, serious thought, Barney enrolled in Swarthmore's class of 1944. It proved a dreadful mistake from the beginning. Barney hated everything about it: his fellow students; its Quaker solemnity; what he perceived as its anti-Semitism; the existence of fraternities; its stultifying atmosphere; and perhaps most unacceptable of all, its expectation that students would actually go to class and complete work, niceties rarely bothered with at Parker. He was even denied the pleasure he hoped to get from football when the coach refused to allow him to play with a kind of face mask he had rigged up out of a wire clothes hanger to protect his glasses. "A hole of nothingness" he complained to his parents, emphasizing his need to get away. They negotiated with him to stay the year, but not before he and a friend, in early February of 1941, managed to borrow a car and take an unauthorized trip as far south as their money would carry them, ending up in Florida. The dean notified Barnet Sr. that his son had disappeared. When their inevitable lack of funds caused them to terminate their adventure and return, the dean welcomed them back, explaining to Senior that nothing like this had ever occurred before and there were no rules about it.

Before Barney left his miserable Swarthmore experience behind him, he had a fateful encounter with a book that turned out to be formative in his life. A classmate tipped him off about a sensational banned novel he should read: Henry Miller's *Tropic of Cancer*, published in Paris but frequently smuggled into the United States. When he learned that it could be obtained in New York, Barney took a train in early May to the city and went to the Gotham Book Mart, Frances Steloff's legendary book store on 47th Street. He approached Steloff hesitantly, asking if the store carried it. When she wanted to know why, he replied that he was a student who had been told he had to have it. Steloff reached under the counter and handed him a copy. Barney fell instantly in love with the book, enamored not of the sex, which he dismissed as basically irrelevant (difficult though it is to imagine a college freshman thinking that), but of Miller's thoroughgoing denunciation of American mediocrity and conformity. Years later, reflecting on the start of his career, he said his goal from "the minute I got into publishing" was to bring *Tropic of Cancer* to an American audience. In the meantime, as a first-year Swarthmore student, the best he could do for Miller was to celebrate the expatriate's criticism of this country in an English paper, dated May 9, 1941, entitled "Henry Miller vs. 'Our Way of Life.'" Bringing together *The Tropic* with writing collected in the *Cosmological Eye*, Barney analyzes Miller's arguments about the degraded nature of American culture. Although he stops short of advocating that we bomb ourselves out of existence, the solution Miller suggests, he emphatically agrees with Miller's position that our current "way of life is not worth defending." Robert Spiller, Barney's American Literature professor, not much impressed with his ardor for Miller's nay-saying, gave him a B- and commented, "Perhaps the jaundice is in the cosmological eye itself, not in the world it sees."

Barney escaped from Swarthmore at the end of his first year. In the following fall, he sought refuge at the University of Chicago after learning that Nancy had also left Vassar to return home. According to Barney, he never attended classes there, compiling a perfect record of incompletes, as most days he would not bother with the university, instead picking Nancy up in his car, where they would spend hours kissing and fondling. Although they had previously conducted a full-fledged sexual affair, Nancy did not want anything so torrid to continue. Barney had no choice but to comply, saying grumpily later that "It was like retrogressing in a way." When he wasn't with Nancy, he joined a left-wing political club on campus whose major task was to sell copies of the communist *Daily Worker* newspaper to the public. Barney immediately became their best salesman, achieving his stellar results through the unique technique of throwing away the fifty copies he was supposed to dispense and providing the club with the requisite proceeds from his own resources.

After a fall semester at Chicago, no more satisfying than what he experienced at Swarthmore, Barney decided to try his academic luck at UCLA, where he thought he would at least be able to indulge his developing interest in film, only to find when he arrived that the university offered no formal film program. Undeterred, he enrolled in various courses and palled around with some left-wing students, unwittingly supplying the FBI, who were busy investigating radical groups, with material for his burgeoning dossier. The outbreak of World War II provided Barney opportunities for fulfillment that he could never find in college—to be his own man, to break free from the supervision of his father, to enact some of the heroic fantasies he entertained about the Spanish Civil War—and he shortly made efforts to involve himself in it. The Marine Corps turned him down because of his flawed vision, as did the Royal Canadian Air Force. He thought about the merchant marine, but his father judged it "insufficiently respectable." Finally, in October 1942, he drove to Chicago to enlist in the army, which, Barney observed, would take anybody who could walk.

Basic training with an infantry unit in Oregon did not bode well for a distinguished military career. Barney did not excel at taking orders or fitting in with the others. "I was not easy to get along with. I argued. I did not always clean my rifle properly. I insulted people. I laughed in their faces. I did not stand at attention properly." But he survived, next going to an officer's training program at Camp Lee, Virginia, before being shifted around to various other bases in the south. Although Barney thought the army held out the promise of immunity from his father's control, it didn't prove that simple. With his money and connections, including, for example, his friendship with James Roosevelt, FDR's son, Barnet Sr. could wield considerable power, even in the military. Father didn't want son to risk his life and arranged the quartermaster corps for him, arguing that Barney could have both the satisfaction of serving in the army while sitting out the war safely in an office somewhere. Not partial to dying, Barney nevertheless felt that such an assignment, devoid of the risk he needed to authenticate his self-image, would not accomplish anything. "I did not want to be in the quartermaster corps. I did not want to get killed either, but my position in the army had to at least indicate a possibility of danger. Otherwise, what was the point of the whole thing?" After an initial stint in the quartermaster corps, where he was commissioned second lieutenant in September 1943, Barney forged a compromise with his father that Barnet Sr.'s influence could deliver: Barney would be transferred out of the quartermaster corps to study combat photography, first in Boston, then at the Army Motion Picture School in Long Island, which featured noted film directors John Huston and Frank Capra as temporary instructors. Barney had a splendid time in film school. He stayed at a comfortable hotel on the east side in New York City and during the day worked at the filmmaking he enjoyed. At night, liquor and girls took his mind off the movie business. On August 29, 1944, second lieutenant Rosset shipped out to India as an officer in the 164th Signal Photo Company. He found his New Delhi assignment boring, wanting to get instead to China where he could witness fighting "before it was too late. It was my chance to get in on the glamorous side of war." After several frustrating months in India, through the paternal meddling he both decried and depended on, he finally made it to Kweiyang.

China had occupied a central role in Barney's imagination ever since he had read two books about the country while still at the Parker school: Edgar Snow's *Red Star Over China* (which he went on to republish at Grove) and Andre Malraux's *Man's Fate*. Barney claimed the two books represented different sides of him: Snow's historical account of Mao's long march, the socially conscious part, concerned with injustice and the need to resist fascist oppression; and Malraux's novel of intrigue and betrayal, the romantic Barney, caught up in fantasies of heroic action and self-sacrifice. China served, in a sense, as a substitute for the Spanish Civil War. He loved his Chinese experience, feeling free, responsible, and competent: "I had my laboratory and I could work in it day and night. I could go to restaurants. I could lay a girl. I could have the tremendous excitement of driving out into parts of China almost devoid of Americans. It was the top of the curve in my army career."

Barney took pictures, searched for missing army personnel with Theodore White, later of *The Making of the President* fame, and got to know some of the tough OSS types who were engaged in demolition and sabotage behind the Japanese lines.

Barney's single most daring act, which he admitted himself was accidental, involved photographing the recently captured Liuchow Airport. Barney and two others drove around the airport in a jeep, snapping photos, totally unaware that the Japanese had placed mines near the various bomb craters pockmarking the runway. Through no skill of their own, they managed to avoid being blown up. The totally adventitious nature of the experience notwithstanding, Barney thought he should receive some recognition for it. He convinced first lieutenant Passantino, his immediate superior and roommate, to whom Senior had previously written a letter asking that he look after Barney, to recommend him for the Bronze Star, "for meritorious service in the face of the enemy." Much to

27

Barney's displeasure, the recommendation was turned down by the commanding general, leaving Barney complaining futilely that the Star was awarded even to some who never left their desk chairs.

With the war over in 1945, Barney found himself stuck, first in China, then India, with nothing to do. He longed to get home, and turned to the source of getting all things done—his father—to make it happen. Barnet Sr. pulled the strings he had at his disposal, but the army remained indifferent to his son's plight. Even his mother entered the act, soliciting a letter from the psychiatrist Leo Kaplan to the secretary of war in October 1945, explaining the deleterious effects on her health caused by the prolonged absence of her only child. She "was referred to my office," Dr. Kaplan writes, "because of a severe dermatitis and other symptoms indicating emotional disturbance. The latter consisted of the usual manifestations of anxiety (e.g., tremulousness, loss of appetite, restlessness, inability to concentrate, sleeplessness and periods of crying). The rash was obviously a neurodermatitis." Dr. Kaplan concludes that in his opinion the only viable therapy for her depressed condition would be the return of her son. Whether in response to the medical appeal or the simple grinding to a conclusion of the military bureaucracy, early in December Barney was put on a ship in Karachi, bound for New York.

Coming back to the United States, Barney also encountered an unpleasant family—or more precisely paternal—situation. Prior to leaving for India in the summer of 1944, while a student in the army film program in Astoria, he met Gale

Barsh, an aspiring writer from South Carolina. Though she was originally somebody else's blind date, she and Barney were instantly attracted to each other and began a passionate affair. Gale excited him sexually as he had never been before: "She was the first girl in my life with whom I had a close relationship who really enjoyed fornication. I could not get enough of it. It was like discovering a new world. She wanted sex as much as I did. I was no longer the male beggar." Much of Gale's past was shrouded in vagueness—Barney didn't really know her age (she claimed to be twenty-two, the same as Barney), or anything about her family, or even whether she was a virgin (as she assured him)—but lust carried the day and Barney resolved to marry her. Before he was sent off to India, the two drove to Michigan to visit his parents at their summer home. Barney's father was not only not impressed, he became highly suspicious of the woman who seemed intent on capturing his young son. When Barney deployed to India, Senior launched an investigation. The results were gratifying for the father, if terminally awful for the son. Gale turned out to be either twenty-seven or thirty, but certainly not twenty-two; she had been married and divorced; had never gone to college, as she had suggested; and according to Claude Thompson, the DC lawyer who reported to Senior, that while it was impossible to document with absolute confidence that either the Brickies or the Barshes (the two lines of Gale's family) "have Negro blood in their veins," he was sure they did. "Aside from the mixture of Negro and other undesirable blood, I am convinced that the Barshes and Brickies are a mongrel race and have gone to seed. If your son

29

should get beyond your control and again meet Gale and marry her, I feel sure that he would soon become sick of it all."

Outraged by this intrusive behavior, Barney initially tried to stand firm, writing to his father in September, while still abroad, "I intend to get married as soon as I get home. And that means immediately, not in six months, nor in one month, but immediately. Investigation of Gale will only make you dislike each other, and if that is the way you want it, then that's the way you want it but I think that is a very poor and stupid way of doing things." But resisting his father never came easily to Barney, and besides, the damage had been done. Barney was upset less by the allegations of Gale's mongrel ancestry than the lies regarding her age. "I spent more time on the age problem than on all the other accusations combined. I figured out over and over again how old she would be when I got home, what her age would be when she finished college."

In light of the damning evidence of her dishonesty, he could not maintain the conviction that they should marry. Senior had triumphed once again. Barney understood the difficulties he faced in trying to assert himself against him: "My father had accomplished what he set out to do. . . . Yet I resented his interference. He had demonstrated his superior will again. He had channeled my love life as he had my army life. I did not want to recognize his authority. . . . He was enforcing his anti-Negro sentiment on me, and I bowed under it, but not gracefully." The three years in the army had not essentially changed anything. Barney remained infantilized by his father. When the steamer from Karachi docked in New York, second lieutenant

Rosset was mortified to discover his father had arranged for his immediate departure from the ship, rather than leaving him alone to disembark with the others in his turn. Like a camp trip, he reflected, where if you know the director your child can get special privileges. "I felt insignificant, a masquerader in an army officer's uniform." It was a feeling against which he would struggle for much of his adult life.

2
JOAN AND BARNEY

When Barney returned to the United States, he headed straight to Chicago, arriving in time to celebrate New Year's Eve with friends at Tin Pan Alley, a bar he liked. In the midst of the drinking and revelry, he suddenly glimpsed the woman destined to become "[a]rguably the most important person in my life." Joan Mitchell, his former Parker schoolmate, who would develop into one of this country's most distinguished abstract expressionists, came walking down the stairs from the ladies' room, "And this weird idea came into my head," he later wrote, "that I was going to get married to her." Three years older than Joan, Barney had been friends with her at Parker and dated her occasionally, though they had not been romantically involved. When Barney had picketed *Gone with the Wind*, Joan accompanied him.

Joan came from a prominent Chicago family. "Jimmie," her father, a talented amateur artist and elegant society's favorite dermatologist, had a thriving medical practice. "A syph and skin man" who knew Al Capone, she once explained to a rapt Barney, "because he was treating him for syph." Joan's mother, Marion Strobel, was a poet and for five years an associate editor of *Poetry* magazine. Joan disappointed Jimmie both because she wasn't the son he had wanted for a brother to Sally, his first daughter, and because she didn't share his political and social views. He stood well to the right of the right-wing "America Firsters," she noted, in addition to being a fervent anti-Semite, of the sort that dismissed FDR as a "kike." But he encouraged her artistic gifts from early on, going with her to museums and urging her to sketch, and took pleasure in her athletic achievements as a ranked figure skater.

Like Barnet Sr. with Barney, Jimmie opted to pursue school prestige for his daughter rather than the politically conservative values he esteemed by sending Joan to Parker, that hotbed of leftist thought. Unlike Barney, however, Joan did not find happiness there. She wasn't interested in politics; she didn't like the radical proselytizing that so delighted Barney. In English class she resented having to learn about communism instead of Shakespeare. The teachers did not like her arrogance and contentiousness, and she had few friends among the students. She hated her father's fierce bigotries at home, while at school, she said in an interview, "they didn't like me because they were communists and they thought I came from a WASP background, which I did. I just couldn't win so to hell with it." At one point, consumed by her interests in skating and painting, she spent so little time in school that Parker considered throwing her out. In the face of considerable opposition, Joan's art teacher came to the rescue, arguing vociferously that her talent merited keeping her. Joan stayed but could never understand the affection people like Barney maintained for the place. Whereas Barney felt altogether nourished and protected at Parker, she felt trapped, belonging nowhere.

Barney did not find her particularly attractive during their time at Parker. In contrast to the lithe Nancy, he reflected, she had none of the grace or agility of a ballerina, being built more like a college fullback. But his epiphany in Tin Pan Alley changed all that. For reasons that he could never fully explain, Joan had suddenly become the woman for him: "My love for Joan," as he put it, "was not like my love for Nancy Ashenhurst. There was not the mad wild longing for her. But Joan was sexually sophisticated, an achiever, and someone I wanted to make my life with." They started going out together, and it rapidly blossomed into an intense romantic relationship. Joan had attended Smith for two years after graduation from Parker but had recently left to study at the Chicago Art Institute, determined to make herself into an important painter. Barney, lacking any specific direction beyond a generalized sense that perhaps he could be a writer, knew that he ought to acquire a college degree. Following his discharge from the army early in February, he enrolled in the University of Chicago. Without Nancy to snuggle with in his car, he actually attended classes.

At the same time, perhaps stimulated by his experience in China in which he came to detest the Nationalist forces led by Chiang Kai-shek, whom he thought did nothing to resist the Japanese, admiring instead the communists who courageously fought against them, he joined the Communist Party. He did so not out of any desire to overthrow the US government but because of his "interest in the solutions it offered of economic, social, and political problems," as he wrote in a 1957 deposition for a passport. The intellectual flirtation didn't last long. Barney rapidly became disaffected with the Party's rigidities and antidemocratic methods. After attending about twenty meetings, sometime in August of 1948 he ended his membership. Before leaving, however, while still in the first blush of Communist enthusiasm in 1946, he helped organize a team for Chicago's intramural football league composed largely of ex-GIs. Under his leadership they decided to call themselves "The Marxists." The term was too much for the patriotic American boys who made up the fraternities. Putting together a team of younger, faster players in better shape than the "Marxist" veterans, they soundly trounced them in the playoff game for the league title.

Barney admired Joan's talent and ambition, but they made his uncertainty about himself all the more painful. Going to college and seeing Joan were life-giving, but they couldn't still the disturbing questions that plagued him about his future. Without his father to take care of him, how could he manage on his own? What could he do? His training as a combat photographer and his interest in movies suggested filmmaking as

a possible answer. And when a friend of his father's suggested
he speak to the head of a film production company he knew
in New York, he immediately went to meet him. Appreciat-
ing that Barney came from a wealthy family, Harry Kapit of
General Films welcomed him enthusiastically. He described
as attractively as possible the company's activities. They
made short films and distributed others. Currently they were
considering a proposal for a film about racial discrimination,
tentatively entitled *Candle in the Wind,* which had been sent
to them from a group at Antioch College. For ten thousand
dollars, he would give the project to Barney. Nothing could
have delighted Barney more than exposing racial prejudice in
America. His gnawing concern was only that perhaps somebody would put the money down before he could. He needn't
have worried: Barnet Sr. endorsed the undertaking; the film
was his to make.

Excited about going to New York to open the office of his
fledgling company, to be called Target Films, he understood
that he first had to finish school and work out future plans with
Joan. He graduated from Chicago's two-year PhB program in
December 1946 and made arrangement to go to New York.
But, perhaps at his father's behest, not before he sought some
professional advice about how best to employ his talents. The
results of the vocational testing from the Institute for Psychological Services of Illinois Institute of Psychology listed his
aptitudes in the following order:

Artist

Musician

Tangible Goods Salesman
Intangible Goods Salesman
Advertising
Lawyer
Author-Journalist
There was no mention of documentary film producer.

Eager to explore the New York painting scene and escape from the Mitchells, Joan agreed to join Barney as soon as she completed her studies at the Art Institute, which she did in June. When Joan got organized to leave her Chicago home, Barney drove back to get her. "He pulled up his fancy station wagon, in the middle of the night," Joan recalled. "And I took all my books and everything else, left a note, and bye-bye. And we drove to New York. That's how I left home. He drove me with my books and my paints."

They moved into an apartment at 1 Fulton Street in Brooklyn owned by Teru Osato, a dear Japanese-American friend and sometime lover of Barney's from the Parker school, whose sister, Sono, had a distinguished career as a dancer with Ballet Russe and later with the American Ballet Theatre. Barney liked them both and corresponded with both in 1943–44. The letters encouraged one vigilant investigator, always concerned about Barney's political loyalties, to include in his FBI dossier the damning entry that during the war he had written to "two Japanese whores" suspected of being spies.

While Joan continued painting, supported by a fellowship from the Art Institute, Barney rented an office at 1600 Broadway, in the same building as Kapit's General Films, and set about his new career. Despite his wartime experience as a combat photographer and head of an army photographic unit, he recognized that he needed some professional help. Gale Barsh, with whom he had remained in contact, introduced him to Leo Hurwitz, a committed left-wing filmmaker with imposing credentials: he had made, in 1942, the powerful docudrama, *Native Land*, with Paul Robeson as singer and narrator, criticizing the union-busting corporations in their effort to subdue the trade union movement. Barney later called him "one of the most intelligent people I have ever met in my life."

Barney discussed his vision of the film with Hurwitz, who accepted his offer to direct and edit it. Instead of *Candle in the Wind*, it would be called *Strange Victory*, referring to the distressing fact that having defeated Hitler in World War II, the United States now found his racist thinking to be on the rise in this country. In place of the Antioch faculty responsible for the original conception, Barney and Hurwitz chose their own writer, Saul Levitt (who would go on to write the stage and screen versions of the *Andersonville Trial*) for the narrative. The combination of a knowledgeable director with strong ideas about the nature of the project and an inexperienced producer with different ones proved problematic from the start. Barney wanted a spare, twenty-minute documentary with a sharp focus on American discrimination against minority groups, particularly blacks. Hurwitz had in mind a feature film of over an hour with a broader embrace, what Barney would later call "variations on a theme, a Bach chorale." It was an unequal struggle. Barney, who admitted he was a lousy chess player because he could never think more than one move ahead, couldn't keep up with Hurwitz's determination to make a longer film. Barney came to detest him and never spoke to him after the film was shown. He lagged behind Hurwitz's dexterity in expanding the subject matter, vainly trying to rein him in and impose his own sense of austerity. When *Strange Victory* finally opened in September 1948, Barney despaired that his original conception of a twenty-minute short had metastasized, under Hurwitz's maneuverings, into four, twenty-minute films, with all the repetition and structural clumsiness of such an awkward form.

As Barney fought with Hurwitz for artistic control, Joan decided her artistic development required that she take her traveling fellowship to Paris. Barney didn't want her to go away, and certainly not without him, but he couldn't desert the film, despite the agonies it caused him: "But this film is like a rope around my neck, strangling the life out of me," he wrote to Joan, "and it has become a living thing I hate, and wish I had never seen or thought of it, and I would like to drown it, like an unwanted child gotten rid of in the dark of night." She left in late June. Barney planned to join her after the movie was completed and shown.

Approaching the end of the actual filmmaking in April, Leo and Barney began to think about publicity. Leo recommended the firm of Friedberg and Katz and sent Barney to negotiate with them. They agreed to the project, but besides billing Target Films on a regular basis did practically nothing else. Leo had expected them to get big names, like Joe Louis and Eleanor Roosevelt, to see the film in preview and rave about its importance, but that never happened. Several brief mentions in newspapers were the best Friedberg and Katz could produce. A showing in July for the trade press did not generate much enthusiasm. Several reviewers criticized its length, and *Variety*, while admiring its socially laudable point of view, noted that it consisted mostly of old newsreel clips edited into a documentary.

The responses were not the sort to entice distributors. No one thought it would make money, and no one wanted to take the risk. Barney finally found Sam Siritzsky of Siritzsky International, owners of the Ambassador Theater on 49th Street west of Broadway. Skeptical that the film would ever be successful, Siritzsky drew up a contract that would protect the company from serious losses. The opening was set for some time in late September.

Several weeks before the scheduled general release, Barney and Leo began showing the film to assorted organization leaders in the hope that they would recommend it to their membership. People came and watched, but almost no interest followed. Perhaps the nicest response to *Strange Victory* came from the important black intellectual W. E. B. DuBois, who saw it on September 22: "You have visualized, made gripping and even terrible many of the facts which I have sought to put in cold prose during my life. I only hope that the public will have courage to see *Strange Victory*." In an attempt to attract an audience, Barney went all out: unemployed actors and Broadway loiterers crisscrossed the city distributing half-price tickets to the Lower East Side, to Harlem, to labor unions and universities; advertising appeared in all the major New York papers and the foreign press; even one-minute radio blurbs in Yiddish were broadcast several times a day.

As Barney continued to hear criticism of the film's length, he resorted to a desperate measure. The night before the official opening, and without Leo knowing about it, Barney engaged Sidney Meyers, a talented editor friend of Leo's, to cut the film, which then ran about ninety minutes. It was an extremely difficult task, both for its rushed nature and the fact that Meyers had to synchronize his cutting with the musical score, but he managed to do it. Barney later said that he and Leo never discussed the shortening.

In its final form, the film, approximately seventy-three minutes long, consists mostly of stock footage—both stills and newsreels—with about five minutes of synchronized sound and ten of footage actually shot for it. Broadway actors Alfred Drake, Muriel Smith, and Gary Merrill provide voice-overs and some dramatic recreations. It opened on a warm, sunny Friday, September 24. Barney sat in the theater, waiting for the customers, but they never appeared in any number. The manager of the Ambassador told him not to worry, first days of new films were frequently that slow. Saturday, however, revealed no appreciable improvement. Barney began handing out cheap-rate tickets during the day to those he encountered on Broadway and 49th Street, emphasizing blacks mostly, as the film focused on their problems in depth. Still, practically no one came into the theater. The manager, ever the optimist, said that people would show up in the evening, after the Yankees game. They didn't. By Saturday night, Barney was thoroughly depressed, particularly when the reviews began coming in, talking about the film's choppiness and incoherence, which extended not just to the images but the commentary as well. The *Daily News* attacked it for perpetrating left-wing propaganda. Barney had held out hope for an article about the film that Leo had been asked to write for the New York *Star*. But rather than extolling the achievement of *Strange Victory*, it turned out to be primarily about Leo's family and the inspiration that led him to make the film.

Despondent, Barney retreated to his hotel room, "almost physically sickened by the lack of business, the bad review, and Leo's article. . . . I broke down and cried and cried. . . . I felt isolated, a failure, and I wanted to annihilate myself. But it was the climax of my *Strange Victory* trip. Then I began to feel better. I stopped sobbing, dried my eyes, and staggered back over to the theater. I knew. The run was a disaster."

Sunday was even worse. Those few who actually saw it on Saturday were part of its largest audience. Nothing more could be expected: the film's admirable intentions could not transcend its flawed execution. Every penny of the $80,000 Barnet Sr. had put into the project was gone. On Sunday night, Barney went to the theater to meet his assistant, Allen Adler (no relation to Alfred), who would go on to embezzle more than half of the small fee Barney later received from a sale to the Czechoslovakia State Film company. Adler was not there but left a note for him at the box office. Echoing a line from the film's narration, which said, "War is an experience marked non-transferable," Adler had written, "Bad business is an experience marked non-transferable. I can't take it any longer." Barney laughed hysterically until tears started to flow. He regarded this as perhaps the most delicious moment in the whole sad saga of the film.

Barney's absorption with *Strange Victory* did not diminish the intensity of his feelings for Joan. Nor hers for him. Letters of mutual longing flowed back and forth between them—Barney unhappy that he let her go abroad, Joan urging him not to be miserable and to come to Paris as quickly as possible. She promised him, with her painterly imagination, that "we'll go swim in a blue sea—and fuck on the yellow sand." The salutations in her correspondence were various and affectionate—"Dear Bubble," "Dear Skinny," "Dear Bernie," "Dear Sweetie Pie,"—but one in particular spoke tellingly of Barney's sense of self at the moment and perhaps even some part of Joan's view of him as well: "Dear Schmuckie." Joan's protestations of love were important to Barney, although they couldn't obviate the despair he felt over what he considered the failure of his first adult undertaking: "I am rather like a mediocre child graduating from high school, no special abilities or interests, geared to go to some cheap third rate college and come out of it a fifth- rate accountant or pharmacist," he confessed to Joan, "only I won't even do that well because I have been out of high school for eight or nine years, and I have no more inside me now than I did then. . . and the future seems full of nothing."

Deeply miserable, despite Joan's exhortation not to be, Barney packed up his film and went off to see her in November.

The torrid nature of their reunion did not brighten Joan's cramped, damp Paris apartment and certainly didn't change the toxic imbalance that, while Joan was actively pursuing the life she loved, Barney still didn't know what to do about his, having permanently discarded the fantasy that he might be a filmmaker. Joan painted and Barney dithered, trying to become a writer. A Parisian high point occurred when the dancer Sono Osato, one of the two "Japanese whores" Barney had kept in touch with during the war, introduced Barney and Joan to Gene Kelly and all went dancing at the famous Le Bal Nègre.

In early December, Joan and Barney were invited to Czechoslovakia to present *Strange Victory* at the Karlovy Vary film festival. With its uncompromising left-wing perspective and dissection of American racism, it became an instant favorite, winning first prize and enabling Barney to sell a copy to the state film company. But though the film was admired, Barney and Joan found little else to like about the Communist regime. When they first arrived, the authorities tried to confiscate Barney's bottle of cognac (they failed, as Barney insisted, no cognac, no film), and nothing much improved after that. Barney and Joan were dismayed by the dreariness and uniformity of it all, the absence of any genuine interest in serious art. After several unpleasant weeks, they had enough. "Let's be bourgeois pigs," Barney announced to a compliant Joan, "and go back to Paris."

Their enthusiasm to be in Paris didn't make the French weather any nicer or Joan's apartment any less drafty, and soon she came down with a serious bronchitis. "Go south," the doctor advised. With Sono's help, they found a villa for rent in Le Lavandou, a seaside resort commune in southeastern France, and drove to sunny Provence in January. Joan resumed painting, gradually breaking away from the social realism that Barney had tried to cajole her into adopting to explore a more abstract style. Joan and Barney had argued for several years over her failure to develop her political consciousness (and accompanying technique) to deal with the progressive concerns that he found appropriate, but now he began to appreciate the fruitful direction in which she was evolving as an artist. Seeing her paint, he came to understand that he had been waging an ill-advised battle. He took great pleasure when she finally emerged as an acclaimed abstract expressionist.

Barney's growing admiration for Joan's work only dramatized his frustrating inability to move forward in his own life. Whereas filmmaking and writing once vied with each other as career possibilities, the trauma of *Strange Victory* had eliminated the former from consideration, leaving him floundering about with the thought that perhaps he could be a novelist, something he had sporadically entertained since entering the Parker School. Unfortunately, Barney suffered from the incurable condition afflicting many young, literate people wishing to be writers: chronic absence of talent. His poetry and various short story attempts never suggest a gift, hidden or otherwise, that could allow him to be a successful author. But Barney aspired nevertheless, particularly without any other plausible or appealing options to examine. So when he wasn't moping, sleeping, playing tennis (passionately, employing two forehands), or staring vacantly out the window, Barney sat down to outline what he described as "a novel of our times." Set in America, from 1945 to the present (1949), it would deal with the main character's leaving the army, trying to decide what to do in the civilian world, and finally arriving at the need to stop and reevaluate. It is the story of "an upper middle-class American male, second-generation money, part Jewish, part Irish, no roots in either one"—wracked with guilt over wanting to help the people but being tied to the father's wealth, caught in the bourgeois way of life while being committed to left-wing ideals. He suffers from the feeling of "never having done anything, of getting everything from father, yet repudiating it, not being able to continue his business, and just as much not be able to strike out alone, and thus arriving at a standstill."

A portrait of Barney, in short, with all the emotional complications leading up to his being stuck in Le Lavandou, not knowing what his next move should be. In his notes for the novel, Barney discusses the different narrative voices he might employ (two), the different literary forms he might include, the need for detailed research, the importance of a thorough outline. With all the novelistic blather about form and structure—"Thus every subjective situation must have its objective counterpoint. There must be a constant interaction of the political and economic and cultural problems with the subjective problems of the characters, thus there will be two types of objective situations . . ." it is clear that this project, so freighted with ideas and aspirations and autobiographical baggage, could never possibly be written. It ends where it begins: with the twenty-seven-year-old Barney trying to map out a future for himself, paralyzed in confusion and doubt.

By the summer it had become clear that Le Lavandou, with all its beauty and charm, had nothing left to offer Barney—or for that matter, Joan, who began to feel the need to plunge back into the active New York art scene. Barney understood that one step he could take to reinvigorate his life immediately would be to enact the vision he had upon first seeing Joan in Tin Pan Alley and marry her. He had, in fact, been trying to do this for some time, but Joan refused. Barney's tenacity, however—a friend once called him a bulldog, another a pit bull—did not crumble in the face of her rejections. He continued his pursuit, explaining how his financial and emotional support would help her. He would expedite her return to New York—she had more or less run out of her fellowship money—and even take back all the canvases she had completed in France, but only if they were married. Joan was not really the marrying kind: too tough, too independent, too ambitious to find happiness in a conventionally sanctioned relationship. Commenting on her prickliness, which he actually found appealing, the poet John Ashbery declared, "She had a knack for putting you ill at ease immediately." Patricia Albers, her biographer, writes that Joan knew she was really not ready for marriage "in the deep sense." But his insistence and ardor were hard to resist. As well, no doubt, as her rather more calculating appraisal about how his money might benefit her career. In an act they both came to regret, she consented to be his wife. They were married in

Le Lavandou on September 10, 1949, and shortly afterwards departed for New York, traveling first class on the S.S. Atlantic. Displaying the economic power attributable to Barnet Sr., Barney paid $960 dollars for their passage, almost half the value of Joan's total Art Institute fellowship. And as he promised, he also handled the shipment of her paintings, ferrying them by rowboat to the SS Atlantic, anchored offshore.

3

THE YOUNG PUBLISHER

The freshly married couple stayed initially at New York's Chelsea Hotel, famous for its august clientele of artists, writers, and musicians, on West 23rd Street, later moving to what Barney called a "dollhouse," a tiny apartment on West 12th Street, and then to the top of a brownstone on 9th Street. Joan immersed herself at once not just in her painting, but in the Greenwich Village art scene, whose social center was the Cedar Tavern at 24 University Place. There Joan smoked, drank, and talked painting with Jackson Pollock, William de Kooning, Franz Kline, and others, determined to break into the largely all male preserve of the developing abstract expressionist movement. Although outside the painting culture, Barney enjoyed the life of the Cedar, insisting he always found artists to be more interesting than writers. And as he by this time had fully accepted Joan's judgment that these were America's great painters, he was happy to be in their presence. Barney attributed the refinement of his esthetic judgments solely to Joan's tutelage. For him, her word was law.

Barney's return to New York did not provide any respite from his creative frustrations. Still entertaining the thought that perhaps he might be a writer after all, he struggled to find something to say and the discipline to sit in front of the type-writer to try to say it. Neither came easily—or at all. "A week of decision," he notes in his journal in the fall of 1950. "After years of meandering, years of no decision, I dare to say that there can be a decision, let alone a week of decision. The deci-sion involved is whether or not to continue to consider writing as a serious future possibility for myself or to relegate it to the dreams unfinished category. . . . Either I achieve a satisfactory work discipline, commencing this week, or I discard the idea of serious writing and turn to another field."

For the blocked, tormented writer, it can be difficult to give up excoriating the self for failure to produce: "If I wish to utilize what strength I have left, to turn it to some positive feeling, what must be done. . . . The answer is sitting in front of my stupid face. WORK WORK WORK WORK WORK. . . . This has gone on long enough. Say it again. No more. No more. Start work. Enough of this shit. What do you want to do. . . . While I am waiting for my 'call' to arrive, why can't I write?. . . . At the bottom of this page, I am going to stop this meandering. . . . When I can't write I will read and when I can't read I will write. I will analyze, think through these things, set my own standards. Fuck the rest of the standards. Where are mine? HERE THEY COME."

Despite his efforts to invoke them, the standards never did arrive, the subconscious flow he was counting on never started up. He felt condemned to failure according to the deadline established by Somerset Maugham, a writer he admired, who held that if you haven't shown promise before thirty, you never will. Barney saw that time was running out: "I am twenty-eight, going on twenty-nine. Nineteen months to go," he calculated in November of 1950, "and not one good story yet. Several books read, many scraps of writing, a little promise, and no more. It won't get me ever [to] the great divide. Twenties to thirties will stop me in Mr. Maugham's book, unless there is a great change."

Barney's anguish as he saw the hourglass running down did not blend well with Joan's growing absorption with her career. If writing wouldn't work, Barney thought that perhaps he might be rescued from his paralysis by a job at the UN. He made a serious effort in 1950 to land a position. But even with his father's connections and the support of Clark Clifford, in Barney's words, one of Truman's "top guys," nothing developed for him. Their marriage began to deteriorate, the two tangling increasingly with one another, privately as well as publicly. "Joan and I were sinking," he recalls sadly, "much as I desired to stay with her. She was very confrontational and combative, and . . . it was impossible to maintain an intimate relationship with her." John Gruen, a friend of both who worked at Grove for a year, writes that he thought his "function was to bear witness to their endless fights." He remembers one evening in which he and his wife, Jane Wilson, had invited the Rossets for dinner in their newly decorated apartment with freshly painted white walls. During the meal, Barney, who was fastidious about keeping slim, cautioned Joan not to have a second helping because she was "getting fat around the middle." In a rage, Joan grabbed a ripe tangerine from the fruit bowl in the middle of the table and flung it violently at Barney's head. Barney ducked, allowing the tangerine to splatter against the formerly immaculate wall: "Thus began one of the more memorable of their many fights, with a barrage of four-letter words filling the air, mercifully replacing the tangerines."

In an effort to save the marriage, the two sought couples therapy. It came to nothing very quickly when the therapist suggested Joan draw pictures about the feelings Barney induced in her, a proposal Joan found ludicrous. And while there were genuine feelings, even if Joan chose not to render them into images on paper, she developed even stronger feelings for Mike Goldberg, a charming, darkly handsome, titillatingly disreputable artist with a highly evolved capacity for lying, whom she met a year or so after arriving in New York. She fell instantly under his spell, attracted to him not just sexually, but also intellectually, to his passionate commitment to painting, every bit as fierce as Joan's, something Barney, the art-outsider, could not share with her. Marriage to Barney proved no impediment to her hunger to be with her lover; in the spring of 1951, Joan moved her studio out of the 9th Street apartment with Barney to West 10th Street, the better to paint and live her life without her husband's interference. Although she continued to see Barney, she gradually spent more and more time in her new studio, eventually equipping it with a hot-water heater—permitting her to bathe in the sink—and a cot.

In the midst of her affair with Goldberg and the intensifying dissolution of her marriage, Joan had a casual conversation with a friend that would transform Barney's life and change forever the nature of American publishing. Talking with Francine Felsenthal, a painter and former student with Joan at the Chicago Art Institute, Joan learned that a tiny, impecunious publishing company on Grove Street in Greenwich Village, owned by two partners, was about to close. Francine understood that Barney had access to family money and didn't know what precisely to do with his life. She wondered whether he would be interested in taking over the company. Joan mentioned the idea to Barney and suddenly a career he had never consciously imagined beckoned to him. Barney recalls the decisive suggestion in two different ways. The first: that it struck a resonant chord in him as if it were something he had always been waiting for; the second: that as his movie producing had failed, his writing had come to nothing, and his marriage was in the process of collapsing, he might as well try something new. The truth no doubt lies somewhere in between. If he had never thought about publishing as an adult, he could remember the pleasure he took as a boy, when he would scrape the "G" off the Grosset and Dunlop books he owned and fantasize about running the Rosset company. And on the other hand, less a buried interest coming to the surface than an unanticipated possibility worth exploring: since he lacked any direction in life and liked books but couldn't seem to write them, why not consider publishing them instead?

Whatever the motivation, he responded with alacrity. The co-owners, Robert Phelps and John Balcomb, had published all of three books in the two years since they started the company in 1949. By the time Barney learned about them, they had run out of assets and patience with each other. Both were eager to sell. Barney traveled to Woodstock, two hours north of New York, where Phelps lived, and bought out his share for $1,500. He planned to join with Balcomb but soon found him too odd to endure. He lived in New York, his apartment piled to the ceiling with newspapers and magazines like the home of the legendary Collyer brothers, whose Harlem brownstone, when they died in 1947, was filled with 140 tons of trash. Barney realized that partnership with Balcomb would not be feasible, and instead purchased his portion of the business for another $1,500. So, for $3,000, courtesy of Barnet Sr., he found himself the sole owner of a practically defunct company known as Grove Press with a total inventory of a few hundred copies each of three paperback books: Herman Melville's *The Confidence Man*; *The Verse in English of Richard Crashaw*, a seventeenth-century English poet; and *Selected writings of the Ingenious Mrs. Aphra Behn*, seventeenth-century English poet, playwright, and novelist. Not exactly a promising backlist for a new publisher, as the books seemed to have been selected precisely because they lacked any kind of contemporary audience. The Phelps-Balcomb publishing philosophy was made explicit on the back of each title page: "The function of the Grove Press, as we understand it, is to publish the kind of books that other publishers publish books about—those 'unexpected' masterpieces of the past and present that have been more read about than read simply because they have been hitherto inaccessible to the general reader." Hardly a formula for commercial success, but Barney, with his love of the idiosyncratic, was intrigued, not deterred. He crammed the books from the Grove office into three suitcases and dragged them up the three floors to his 9th Street apartment to figure out how to be a publisher, about which he knew nothing. He immediately exhibited his ignorance by doing, as he said, "exactly the wrong thing." At a time when the market for quality paperbacks was beginning to develop, he ripped the paper covers off his three volumes and replaced them with more costly hard covers, which he in turn ripped off and replaced with different soft covers. An expensive misjudgment, and by no means the last in a publishing career in which business acumen was never his strongest suit.

Shortly after buying Grove, Barney decided to fold his Chicago two-year PhB degree into the quest for a traditional BA. In the fall of 1951, he entered the New School, which agreed to credit him with seventy-five points for his work at Chicago, leaving him with only forty-five to complete for its degree. Barney took courses with many of the eminent faculty who had made their way to the school: Alfred Kazin on the Art of the Novel, Wallace Fowlie on Modern French Poetry, and Stanley Kunitz on The Modern Short Story. He earned a C with the distinguished art historian Meyer Schapiro in his

Founders of Modern Art course. Shapiro seemed puzzled that Barney could have written such an excellent paper on Pointillism and done so badly on the final exam. He unquestionably would have been less perplexed had he appreciated that the paper was actually written by Joan with the help of a professorial friend in the art history department at the University of California in La Jolla.

With his BA in hand and a business career in sight, Barney thought that a law degree might be useful. In the spring of 1952, he enrolled in NYU Law School. He soon noticed that in his contracts course of three hundred students, the professor appeared to be calling primarily on him. When it occurred to him that he was being used as an illustration of how not to study law responsibly, he quit after one semester.

Now that he possessed his own publishing company, the question remained as to whether or not he also possessed a wife. Joan's ardor for Mike had not cooled and Barney, though patiently observing their affair, had no inclination to share her on a long-term basis. Barney put up with as much as he could of her absence but finally insisted, in the spring of 1952, that if she didn't come back to him full-time he would divorce her. Unwilling to leave Mike but also reluctant to cut off her life support from Barney, Joan asked for more time, no doubt hoping she could persuade Barney to accede to the kind of open marriage that the de Koonings had built for themselves. He was adamant about her returning, however, and when she refused he decided to act. In April of 1952, he traveled to Chicago to take advantage of Illinois's liberal divorce laws. He called

Joan from Chicago the night before his court date, giving her the opportunity to change her mind. She urged him not to go through with it but also made clear she wasn't leaving Mike.

The next day, Barney appeared before Judge Julius Hoffman, a friend of his father's, who would later achieve notoriety in presiding over the trial of the Chicago Seven in 1969. Illinois law had a two-year residency requirement before a divorce could be granted. Barney had wanted Barnet Sr. to testify that his son had been living there for the requisite amount of time, but he was too drunk to show up. Judge Hoffman asked Barney how long he had been an Illinois resident, cautioning him that if he lied he would be guilty of perjury. Barney said he understood the warning, assuring him he had been living in Chicago for two years. He also assured him that Joan had left him on September 15, 1950, seven or so months before she actually did. Judge Hoffman then granted the divorce decree on grounds of desertion.

After the divorce, when Barney had gone to Paris and Joan was looking for an apartment in New York, Barney informed her that he was sending a gift of a young Frenchman to replace him. Joan was smitten with the arrival of the Frenchman at the airport—an adorable brown poodle puppy she named George—who helped her negotiate the difficulties of the return to single life.

Liberated by the divorce—which actually came as a relief to them both—Barney focused his energies on rehabilitating the tiny press he had just acquired. Barney's Grove began very much as a hands-on business—with his being the only hands at work. He sold the books to bookstores from his 9th Street apartment, packed them himself, and then carried them down three flights on the way to the Post Office for mailing. The first volume he actually produced, beyond the three he had inherited, was *The Monk*, a bizarre, convoluted Gothic novel written in 1796 by Matthew Lewis, which Phelps and Bolcomb were planning to issue before they sold to Barney. In all its eccentricity, involving, among other things, a woman disguised as a monk who gains access to a monastery, it appealed to him, and he made it Grove's initial publication. As Joan had always liked Henry James, he followed with *The Golden Bowl*.

Running a business, however small and however single-handedly, requires money, and Barney immediately had to confront the reality that at the outset, at least, Grove Press could not be expected to provide the steady source of income needed to sustain it. Ever since leaving the army, Barney had subsisted on allowances from Barnet Sr., with the amount and timing to be decided by him, a situation that had clearly become untenable. Senior had several years earlier established two trust funds for Barney, but in order to keep paternal control over him, had refused to let him know the terms of the trust agreements or the funds they produced. Senior doled the money out as he saw fit, serving to keep his twenty-nine-year-old son "still in the position of a mentally incompetent, or a minor, who receives a monthly stipend, who has no power in the [determining] of its size," Barney protested to his father in April, "and who has no clear idea of where the money is coming from, how much of it there is, and who does not know if this river of gold will continue to flow." Barney stressed that such an arrangement is not only demoralizing to him but in "explicit contradiction to the terms of the trust agreements which must give me some powers." He goes on to emphasize to his father that the expenses he has incurred "are not the result of buying large automobiles, mink coats, diamonds, nightclub sprees or any of the other things which are usually put into the fancy luxury class."

Senior did not appreciate Barney's desire to handle his own affairs and reminded him that he had previously maintained he had the power to cut him off completely from the trust funds if he wished. Barney, in turn, reminded his father that when they had earlier discussed this possibility, Barney had said he would hire a lawyer to "determine whether or not you could do that." The spectacle of son suing father happily did not come about after Senior, with Barney's consent, proposed to discuss the matter with Judge Campbell, an old family friend. Judge Campbell decided that Barney should have access to both information and funds, and the crisis was averted.

Even with the trust fund issue satisfactorily settled, Barney realized from the start that he didn't have the resources to compete with the established publishing houses in offering serious advances for new work by American authors. He would have to limit himself at the beginning to the Phelps-Balcomb strategy of "classic reprints"—Dickens, Thackeray, Austen—in addition to those "unexpected masterpieces" (like *The Monk* and *Aphra Behn*, for example), which carried with them no copyright expense. During the company's first year, as the inventory piled up in Barney's 9th Street apartment and he toiled mightily to package and mail the books by himself, he concluded that this could no longer be an enterprise he ran alone from his own home. So he rented a small suite of offices at 795 Broadway and began to build a staff, starting with his friend John Gruen as publicity director and writer of press releases. Over a beer one night he confessed to Gruen that he had been lonely following his divorce, and wondered if Gruen knew any interesting women for him. Gruen, who had been working at Brentano's, a New York bookstore, said there was a marvelously attractive German sales girl there, Hannelore Eckert, and gave him her number.

Loly, as she was called, was born in Germany and spent the wartime years in Paris, where her father was a major in the German intelligence. When the war ended, she married a man in Germany who later committed suicide; she had a child with him who died after only several months. She came to the United States in 1951. Barney called her, liked her, and lured her away from Brentano's by appointing her sales manager. Loly had no qualifications for such a position, but Barney thought that a beautiful, elegant woman with a soft foreign accent could not go far wrong in representing Grove to bookstore owners and managers. As was the case for many of Barney's whimsical hirings, she learned the job by doing it. On her first sales trip to California, she unexpectedly met the German doctor who had tried to save her child's life in Germany and had subsequently set up his medical practice in Santa Barbara. He asked her to marry him; Loly, attracted to the notion of some kind of secure life after the trauma of the war, said yes, and called Barney long-distance to inform him she was not coming back. Barney told her she couldn't do that. "Do what?" she retorted. "Resign," he said, "Grove needs you." A surreal conversation ensued. Barney argued she couldn't get married and leave Grove. He appealed to her not to make any decision until they had a chance to talk together. She agreed to meet him halfway, in Chicago. Several days later, each arrived. Barney was at his charming, persuasive best, and by the end of their discussion, Loly had consented to give up the doctor and marry him instead. When asked why he proposed under such duress, Barney replied that, given the doctor's offer, what choice did he have? He had to act decisively if he were to retain his sales manager. The two were married in New York in August 1953. Barney had succeeded in keeping Grove's sales manager in place.

His lack of business experience notwithstanding, Barney understood that reprinting the classics was not a formula for building the company. He needed help and advice in navigating the new world he had just entered and sought them in a Columbia University night course—Editorial Practices and Principles of Book Publishing—taught by a revered Random House editor, Saxe Commins. Whatever he learned from the class about practices and principles was less important than his meeting another student in it, the taciturn but talented Don Allen, who became the first editor Barney hired. He would go on to coedit the two first issues of *Evergreen Review* and edit the influential volume, *The New American Poetry*, published by Grove in 1960.

For personal advice, shortly before earning his New School BA, he consulted Wallace Fowlie, his professor of modern French poetry at the school. Fowlie remembers the moment clearly when the "slender, small of stature, boyish looking" Rosset waited at the back of the room until the other students left: "His first words were: 'I want to solicit your help and advice because I have just bought a publishing house and want to choose some French books for my first list.'" Fowlie recommended that he purchase the rights of three French dramatists: Samuel Beckett, the Irishman who wrote in French; Eugene Ionesco; and Jean Genet. According to Fowlie, Barney was not overly enthusiastic about the suggestions initially, though, after bringing Beckett's *Waiting for Godot* to Grove, he soon followed with the other two.

Barney's account of how he came to publish Beckett is somewhat different. In his version, he had originally heard about Beckett from Sylvia Beach, owner of the famous Paris bookstore Shakespeare and Company and the first publisher of James Joyce's *Ulysses*. Beach was a friend of Joan Mitchell's mother, Marion Strobel, from whom she had learned about Barney's new publishing career. Beach wrote to Barney, enthusiastically recommending Beckett. Barney subsequently noticed a small article in the *New York Times* about a performance of *Godot* in Paris. Intrigued, he tracked down a copy (in French) whose power, pain, and macabre humor astonished him. When Fowlie agreed with Beach about the work's greatness, Barney resolved to publish it.

But whether Fowlie told Barney about Beckett or simply endorsed Barney's enthusiasm for Beckett, it is clear that Barney immediately grasped that the enigmatic play of the obscure Irish writer living in Paris and more or less totally unknown in the United States should be made available here. If Grove as a publishing house became famous for one basic principle, it was to pay no attention to the bottom line. For Barney, interesting books should be published, irrespective of their potential to sell. Not a commitment to ensure the financial viability of a publishing company, perhaps, but one which guarantees that the perceived quality of a work trumps niggling fiscal realities. The policy set Grove apart from other publishers. Barney liked *Godot*, and that was all that mattered. In the summer of 1953, he negotiated with the small French firm of Les Editions de Minuit, Beckett's French publisher, and Marion Saunders, Beckett's American agent, for the American rights. In a 1985 interview, Jérome Lindon, the director of the company who sold Barney the rights for $150, stressed that there was little sense then that the play might be successful: "The success of *Waiting for Godot* is miraculous. No one expected it: neither Beckett, nor me, nor Barney, nor anyone. . . . It is certain that Barney did not publish Beckett for commercial reasons." That Barney was not distressed by *Godot* selling 341 copies its first year suggests his disdain for the trivial matter of sales figures. Nor was he discouraged when what would go on to be generally acknowledged as the defining play of the twentieth century had a disastrous US opening at Miami's Coconut Grove

Theater in 1956. The audience's angry bewilderment at the rambling conversation between the seedy Estragon and Vladimir generated the following joke: "Question: Where is the most difficult place in Miami to get a taxicab? Answer: The Coconut Grove Theater after the first act of *Godot*." It wasn't until its Broadway opening several months later that American critics and audiences began to catch up to the originality of Beckett's work.

Barney had worked through friends, agents, and publishers on the way to getting the rights to *Godot*, but by the summer of 1953 he thought it was time to contact Beckett directly. On June 18, he wrote to him for the first time, beginning a warm and loving friendship that endured until Beckett's death in 1989. For Barney, Beckett was his greatest hero and the most important writer he ever published. His admiration was such that over the years he issued every one of his works through Grove, making sure to keep all of them in print, regardless of sales. More personally, he demonstrated his feelings for him by naming his second son Beckett. In his June 18 letter, beyond introducing himself to "Mr. Beckett," Barney wanted to resolve the problem of who would translate *Godot* into English from its French original. There were various possibilities, but, Barney advised, "If you would accept my first choice as translator the whole thing would be easily settled. That choice, of course, being you."

"Dear Mr. Rosset," Beckett replied on the 25th, assuring him that he would undertake the translation of *Godot* himself and leave open the question of how his other novels in French would be handled. But then he raised an issue that presciently anticipated the struggle to which Barney would devote his energy and financial resources, and which would constitute an essential part of his legacy to American publishing in particular and culture in general: his campaign against censorship of any sort. Beckett cautions him,

> With regard to my work . . . I hope you realize what you are letting yourself in for. I do not mean the heart of the matter, which is unlikely to disturb anybody, but certain obscenities of form which may not have struck you in French as they will in English, and which frankly (it is better you should know this before we get going) I am not at all disposed to mitigate. I do not of course realize what is possible in America from this point of view and what is not. Certainly as far as I know such passages, faithfully translated, would not be tolerated in England. I think you would do well to talk to Fowlie about this.

As it turned out, Barney had no trouble with *Godot* and the censors, but Beckett's letter, in making the case for the necessity of free expression, introduces the very concern that would preoccupy Barney throughout his career in publishing.

On September 16, Loly and Barney embarked for Europe on the French liner *Le Flandre* with the intention of seeing friends in England, Loly's family in Germany, and most importantly, Beckett in Paris. They met Beckett at the bar of the Pont Royale Hotel, where they were staying, at six thirty. The notoriously private Beckett had earlier explained that as he had other engagements scheduled, he could only spend forty-five minutes with them. He arrived late, wearing his characteristic trench coat and looking harassed and nervous. The evening started badly, Loly recalls, with awkward silences, until she told Beckett out of desperation how much she had enjoyed reading *Godot*. With that, everybody relaxed and the conversation among the three became warm, friendly, and fun. Beckett's other appointments were forgotten (unlikely that they ever existed), and they went to dinner and then drank at various bars, ending up at one of Beckett's favorites, La Coupole, with Beckett buying champagne at three in the morning.

The forbidding Beckett turned out to be charming and accessible; "Mr. Rosset" and "Mr. Beckett" instantly became Barney and Sam, with Barney becoming not just Sam's American publisher but his agent and dear friend as well. The kindest man he had ever known, Barney declared. (Some years later, when the 1969 Nobel Prize for literature had transformed Beckett from a little-known author into an international celebrity, he and Barney had spent a night on the town drinking in Paris. At the close of the evening, an electrical blackout in the city made it impossible for Beckett to get through the electrically controlled outer door of his apartment building, so the two of them went to Barney's hotel, climbed the seven flights to his room and shared the luxury of his king-sized bed. "Now I could say," Barney subsequently quipped, knowing the distinction such an achievement would confer upon him, "that I had been to bed with Samuel Beckett.")

Getting to know Beckett was the high point of the trip, but Barney also acquired more writers, Genet and Ionesco, among others, as well as the rights to D. H. Lawrence's 1928 translation of Sicilian novelist Giovanni Verga's *The House by the Medlar Tree*, which became, later in 1953, the first Grove book to earn a *New York Times* front-page book review. Less dramatic, but no less significant for the future of Grove, Barney met Richard Seaver, a young American writer and editor, cofounder of the English language literary quarterly *Merlin*, who was working in Paris while completing his doctoral dissertation at the Sorbonne on James Joyce. Barney had read a *Merlin* essay Seaver had written on Beckett and wanted to know more about this young critic who was prepared to confront the difficulties of Beckett's novels, *Molloy* and *Malone Dies*. The two men shared an attraction for the unusual and the avant-garde, and for the pleasures of risk taking. They liked each other immediately, with Seaver vowing to look Barney up should he ever leave Paris for New York. In 1959, when Seaver was working in New York for the publisher George Braziller, Barney convinced him to join in in the excitement at Grove and hired him as editor, where he stayed, an indispensable colleague and eventually editor-in-chief, until 1971.

4
A RADICAL ANOMALY

For a neophyte publisher with little income and less recognition, signing up the peculiar play he had no reason to think would ever sell of a writer practically no one had ever heard of represented Barney at his most brilliantly impulsive. He launched himself into the book business without the burdens of knowing precisely what he was doing or how to do it, trusting only his unshakeable confidence in his ideas and preternaturally sharp intuitions about literary value and innovation. Barney happily embraced his chutzpah: "I have always been and still am a radical anomaly in a basically conservative age," he declared, "politically, esthetically, yes, even sexually. That's what I am all about." While loathing the reactionary stance of New York's mayor Rudolph Giuliani (1994–2001), he admired a political cartoon criticizing the mayor's capriciousness. With

Giuliani depicted holding a gun, the caption reads, "Ready, fire, aim," which Barney thought accurately captured his own decision-making process.

If he lacked the money for big-time advances, he would have to take chances with writers who were not well-known and therefore not being simultaneously pursued by the respectable, buttoned–up publishers he called the "redcoats"—men like Alfred Knopf and Roger Straus. Barney liked to describe himself as an amoeba (though one with a left-wing brain), who could flow fluidly into nooks and crannies where bulkier organisms would not think to explore. Long before others figured it out, in Richard Seaver's words, he "sensed or smelled or thought" that the richest trove of available talent were those relatively obscure European writers who had come to artistic maturity in the decade following the end of World War II, people like Beckett, Robbe-Grillet, Genet, Ionesco, and Duras. Publishing them here, Barney effectively introduced the avant-garde into literary America's consciousness, changing the country's reading habits.

Taking on the challenges of a new business—his "weird aberration," as he came to think of it—and a new wife, he found an appropriately weird setting for both in an East Hampton Quonset hut: the sole American construction of French modernist architect Pierre Chareau, who built it for the painter Robert Motherwell in 1946. Motherwell's decision in 1952 to leave the wilds of East Hampton for an elegant Manhattan townhouse led Barney and Loly to drive out to see the house they had read about in *Harper's*—"this strange-looking thing," as Barney later described it, "stuck in a pile of sand." The two loved it immediately. The agent informed them they could rent it for nine thousand dollars, or buy it for twelve. Later that year, Barney brought Barnet Sr. to see it. His father's response was predictable: "'You bought THAT! You paid twelve thousand dollars for THAT!'"

Barney dreamt of building a Grove community around them and did succeed in conveying several abandoned houses on wheels to East Hampton where he refurbished them and made them available to Grove employees. He even brought a tiny church out to his land and crafted a little theater out of it, called the Evergreen Theatre. His fantasy of running the company entirely from the Quonset hut did not prove viable in the long run, but he managed it for a while, coming into New York twice a week and staying at a hotel in Greenwich Village. He never lost his affection for the house and regretted selling it in 1980 when he needed the money; it didn't occur to him that the new owners would fail to maintain it. But they had no interest either in Chareau or his unique architectural achievement, concerned only for the valuable two-acre lot on which the house sat. They put a price tag on it of a single dollar if someone would remove it to another part of the island. Nobody volunteered, and shortly one old Quonset hut in need of repair was torn down. Barney was heartbroken at its disappearance. "It seems utterly tragic and incomprehensible," he complained to the East Hampton *Star*, "that a homeowner and his architect, supposedly of some cultural sophistication, would find it necessary to destroy a local landmark known for its famous architect, its daring and wonderful design, its justly famous first owner, and for the many other great artists who worked and socialized in it." Afterwards, he found it painful to go past the site on which it once stood.

As Barney continued to build the company and trawl foreign waters for overlooked treasures, he and Loly settled into the second of his unsuccessful marriages. Later, when asked why his first four wives left him (Astrid, his fifth wife was with him at his death), Barney responded with some jocularity that he must have been driven to find women who would walk out on him—satisfying some neurotic need, he speculated. "No, Barney," Astrid corrected him, "you drove them away." More to the point, the center of Barney's life was always and only Barney—a problem for anyone in an emotional relationship with him. If he required the support of women, which his five marriages suggested he did, he also needed to assert his will over them; he could become savagely abusive in the face of disagreements of any sort. Alcohol made confrontations considerably nastier.

Barney's complicated feelings toward women—his love of them and his anger at them—are revealed in the 1949 outline for the autobiographical novel he never wrote. His unnamed protagonist, clearly a Barney persona, reflects on how much he admires and desires women but simultaneously how difficult it is for him to rid himself of a conviction of male superiority. His attraction to women is such that he wants them to be equal to him so that he can be nourished by them but has difficulty believing in the possibility. "One thing he feels is that if women are discriminated against, they will not reach high intellectual levels and thus he will be cut off from communicating with them." He would like to deny his anti-women feeling, but finally he concludes "that in our society it is almost impossible . . . for men not to feel superior to women." The character, then (and perhaps the author as well?), is trapped between his yearning for female equality and an instinctive rejection of the idea: "So XX, at first, will deny vehemently any chauvinism, but actually it will exist in large doses. One thing which will run parallel to this professed and believed idea of equality will be the desire of dominating and hurting women also."

Whatever the etiology, Barney's volatility was not pleasant to experience. Both as husband and as boss, he could be scathing. Marriage carried with it no immunity from personal criticism for wives working at Grove: Barney yelled at Loly in the office every bit as brutally as he did at home. Loly, a Buddhist, developed a unique method of dealing with the office intercom lacerations. When Barney became particularly vituperative, she pulled her meditation pillow out from beneath her desk and set cross-legged on it until the storm passed. Loly delivered Barney's first child, Peter, in 1955, and survived two more years as wife and office assistant before resigning both positions in 1957.

Under Barney's direction, Grove gradually began to be known as the offbeat house that couldn't pay large advances but was willing to publish little-known authors whose works the established companies wouldn't consider. The growth of its reputation as a good place for the avant-garde brought with it more manuscripts of disparate sizes and subjects than Grove had the money or capacity to turn into books. Don Allen, Barney's first editor, whom he hired in 1952, was unhappy at having to turn down interesting submissions because they were either too short or too long to publish as conventional books. Grove had no way, for example, to publish a provocative essay or a few powerful poems. Allen began thinking about creating a magazine, more like a quarterly, which could offer writers an opportunity to display their wares through essays, short stories, poems, and excerpts from longer pieces. He imagined something with a more enduring shelf life than a normal weekly publication, in the format of a trade paperback. He typed up his ideas as to what such a publication might look like and negotiated with Barney about the possibility. Barney was interested, particularly when Allen promised to edit the first four issues for free if Barney would agree.

The result of their discussion was the birth of the *Evergreen Review*, whose first issue came out in 1957. Its aspirations for intellectual seriousness and broad artistic engagement are evident in the initial table of contents: an essay by Jean-Paul Sartre on the aftermath of the Hungarian revolution; a short story by Beckett; an interview with Baby Dodds, famous New Orleans jazz drummer; portions of French novelist Henri Michaux's book *Miserable Miracle*, on the effects of mescaline; photographs by distinguished American photographer Harold Feinstein; fiction by James Purdy; a discussion of *Lady Chatterley's Lover* by Professor Mark Schorer, which was later included as the introduction to Grove's 1959 unexpurgated edition of the novel.

But it was the second number that vaulted *Evergreen* into cultural notoriety. Don Allen, more immersed in the American poetry scene than Barney, had become alerted to the poetic ferment going on in California, where names like Ginsberg, Corso, Ferlinghetti, and (pre–*On the Road*) Kerouac had begun to make their way across the country. The two editors decided to lay claim to the appearance of a new poetic generation with an issue devoted, as a banner splashed across the cover announced, to the "San Francisco Scene." With an essay by poet and critic Kenneth Rexroth extolling, in the magazine's own words, "the exciting phenomenon of a young group in the process of creating a new American culture," *Evergreen* offered to a national audience what was in effect the first collection of the "Beat poets": Gary Snyder, Michael McClure, Kenneth Rexroth, Lawrence Ferlinghetti, Philip Whalen, Josephine Miles, Jack Kerouac, and Brother Antoninus, among others, including what was without question the decade's most important poem, Allen Ginsberg's "Howl." Ginsberg had earlier published it as a pamphlet with Ferlinghetti's City Lights press, where it had been confiscated as obscene and Ferlinghetti and his manager at the City Lights bookstore put on trial for selling it. As Barney had not yet begun his campaign to end censorship laws (which he initiated against the ban on *Lady Chatterley's Lover*), he was not prepared to become entangled with the courts, so he prudently omitted to print the poem's obscene section.

The issue sold out quickly, and Barney, treating *Evergreen* more as a book than a magazine, promptly printed another five thousand. In addition to publicizing the Beats as a group, *Evergreen's* "San Francisco Scene" established Grove, in a sense, as the unofficial publisher of the Beat generation. Barney always felt a close affinity to the Beat spirit, which he personally thought began with the rebellious nonconformity of Henry Miller. "To me, the Beat Generation writers, even if they didn't always see it that way, were also of necessity a courageous political movement and a proud icon for freedom of expression. It was what it was and it was also a part of me." For Barney, the Beat ethos was epitomized in the free spirits of Ginsberg—"the heart and soul of the Beat Generation"—and Kerouac—"its shining star."

After Don Allen left for California two years later, Barney took over as editor, assisted by Seaver, Fred Jordan, and Marilyn Meeker. Until 1971, when financial difficulties caused it to be closed down, *Evergreen* helped spread the Grove brand of radical political ideas and avant-garde writing across the country. It also served as a kind of promotional tool for Grove, enabling Barney to publish work by interesting authors to whom he couldn't immediately offer book contracts: "And it was extremely effective in exactly that way," Barney stressed. "When we published sections of a book, or a play, it was in the hope that we'd get to do the whole thing. And we did get authors in that way, like John Rechy [*City of Night*] for instance." In particular, Barney thought of *Evergreen* as Grove's "political wing," speaking to political issues (or at least Barney's view of them) without requiring the expense and effort of publishing an entire book.

A short list of some of the significant writers and artists of our time who were delighted to publish with *Evergreen*— Albert Camus, Jean-Paul Sartre, Octavio Paz, Beckett, Pablo Neruda, Larry Rivers and Frank O'Hara, Amiri Baraka, Boris Pasternak, Heinrich Böll, Gunter Grass, Jorge Luis Borges, Susan Sontag, Federico Garcia Lorca, Yevgeny Yevtushenko, Paul Goodman, Edward Albee, and Carlos Fuentes, to name a few—suggests the distinction of the magazine's contributors.

Eager to expand its audience, Barney decided in 1964 to change *Evergreen* from the trade book format of 5 ½" x 8 ¼" to that of a glossy magazine, 8 ½" by 11", and its schedule from quarterly to monthly. The quality of the writing didn't change, but the contents did, seeking a broader appeal with cartoons, photographs, more sexual material, pungent political commentary, and even a satirical comic strip—"Phoebe Zeit-Geist"— featuring a bare-breasted heroine. The public welcomed the magazine's new format; it eventually achieved a subscription level of forty thousand and newsstand sales of approximately one hundred thousand.

Barney managed to run into censorship difficulties with the very first issue of the new *Evergreen*, demonstrating his capacity to rouse the ire of America's puritan sensibilities. He had brought back from Paris early in 1964 some prints of nudes taken by the distinguished art photographer Emil Cadoo. He included several of them in issue No. 32 (April–May 1964), as well as one for the cover. The artful nature of the photographs required careful study to detect that they revealed the unclothed female body. A woman working in the plant printing the magazine in Hicksville, Long Island, reported the unsavory material to her husband, a detective on the vice squad, who in turn alerted an earnest district attorney in Nassau County. Just before the printing was to be bound, the police raided the plant and carted off everything to the police station, making a mess of the material. Grove's lawyer, Cy Rembar, promptly instituted a suit against the DA personally for violating Grove's First Amendment rights. Chastened, and not enthusiastic about defending himself in court, the DA returned everything, promising he would not bother the magazine again as long as the editors left him alone. Everyone agreed. The number came out with the Cadoo photos—along with fiction by Norman Mailer, Jean Genet, William Burroughs, Eugène Ionesco, and Robert Musil, poems by Gunter Grass and Michael McClure, and a short story by Rolf Hochhuth, the young German author of *The Deputy*, the controversial play about the role of Pope Pius XII in World War II (also published by Grove). Barney objected that the issue was never bound properly.

The repressive forces of propriety in the 1960s against which Barney fought were not just sexual but political as well. For Barney, in fact, the two were very much one. He understood the profound connection between those who wished to control what Americans were permitted to read and those who wanted to impose their will on every aspect of people's lives. It explains why he was determined to resist the laws against obscenity: "I had a long-standing thing about censorship. To me, the people who were the censors were the ruling class in this country. Look at the people who were against people voting, who were against women, who were against sex—that was a part of my life." Following the run-in with the law over the Cadoo photos, *Evergreen's* next issue featured a poem by Judith Malina that ended with the line, "Fuck the USA." The patriotic printer insisted it be removed. Would it be acceptable if instead the line read, "Fuck the Soviet Union?" Barney inquired. The printer assured him he would have no trouble with such a sentiment. *Evergreen* dismissed that printer and went through several others until locating one sufficiently subversive to be willing to entertain a slur against this country. Number 33 came out with fiction by John Fowles, Jack Kerouac, Jakov Lind, a section of Richard Brautigan's *Trout Fishing in America*, and an essay on writing for the theater by Harold Pinter, among other pieces. It constituted either the high or low point of *Evergreen's* capacity to upset the establishment when House Minority Leader Gerald Ford denounced the magazine on the floor of the Congress for printing a lampoon of Richard Nixon beside the photo of a nude woman.

Although Barney's career as a movie producer did not survive the defeat of *Strange Victory*, he never lost his interest in film. In 1963, he commissioned film scripts from five writers—Beckett, Ionesco, Duras, Pinter, and Robbe-Grillet—with the intention of having Grove find backers to produce them. Of these, the BBC did Pinter's, and Grove did Beckett's. For the only time in his life, Beckett came to New York in the summer of 1964 to work on his twenty-four-minute silent film in black and white. Barney convinced Alan Schneider, Godot's original American director, to direct it, and the distinguished cinematographer Boris Kaufman to film it. Beckett wanted Charlie Chaplin to play its only role, but when Chaplin refused, Beckett settled on Buster Keaton instead. Keaton was more or less broken down at this point in his career and didn't really understand what exactly he was doing or why, but since Schneider was firmly in control of the entire production, it hardly mattered. The film, aptly enough entitled *Film*, is elusive and tantalizing in the best Beckett manner, examining the nature of perception. Beckett's explanation suggests its obscurity: "A movie about the perceiving eye, about the perceived and the perceiver—two aspects of the same man." Beckett judged it an interesting failure.

Barney claimed that if you wanted to know what kind of person he was, you should look at the books he published, which explains a lot, if not exactly everything. It does not suggest, for example, that he was indifferent to the classics of American literature. He would have loved to publish Hemingway and Faulkner, he wryly pointed out, but as they were taken he had to look elsewhere. John Rechy (*City of Night*, 1962) and Hubert Selby Jr. (*Last Exit to Brooklyn*, 1964) were hardly comparable, but they were available and both wrote provocative novels that challenged sexual and social conventions in ways that appealed to Barney.

Join the Underground, Grove-*Evergreen* urged a young, adventurous audience in a 1966 ad campaign that appeared in the *New York Times*, *New York Review of Books*, and the *Village Voice*, among other publications, as well as on posters in the

New York subway system. IF YOU'RE OVER 21; IF YOU'VE GROWN
UP WITH THE UNDERGROUND WRITERS OF THE FIFTIES AND SIX-
TIES WHO'VE RESHAPED THE LITERARY LANDSCAPE; IF YOU WANT
TO SHARE IN THE NEW FREEDOMS THAT BOOK AND MAGAZINE
PUBLISHERS ARE WINNING IN THE COURTS, THEN KEEP READ-
ING. YOU'RE ONE OF US. For such daring, sophisticated readers Grove offered between 1966–68 the sexual blockbusters of
three volumes of the eighteenth-century French libertine and
aristocrat the Marquis de Sade, published in both hardcover
and mass market paperback—*Justine, Philosophy in the Bedroom,
and other writings; The 120 Days of Sodom;* and *Juliette*—and the
two-thousand page, two-volume autobiography rendering the
various erotic exploits of an anonymous English Victorian gen-
tleman, *My Secret Life,* released in 1966.

In an effort to entice people into exploring the wares of
the Grove underground, Barney took full advantage of the
decidedly mainstream academic study, *The Other Victorians*
(1966), written by Professor Stephen Marcus of Columbia
University's English department. Marcus's research, done at
the Kinsey Institute Archives, explores the sexual world of
nineteenth-century England, the world omitted by the great
Victorian novelists. He devotes two chapters to *My Secret Life,*
indicating the centrality of the book to an understanding of
how life was actually lived outside the fictional universes of
Dickens and Thackeray. His scholarly examination provided
a credible cover to those whose sexual curiosity was piqued
by what respectable gentlemen did when they weren't being
respectable. Readers could receive not only an erotic charge

but at the same time enhance their sociological and historical knowledge of Victorian England. Barney made sure to tie Marcus's scholarship to the book's promotion. The Evergreen Book Club, which Barney had started early in 1966, offered *The Other Victorians* for free to club members who bought the two-volume hardcover edition. By 1969 Grove had sold nearly 750,000 paperback copies of *My Secret Life*.

While Grove's prominent underground works included, in the mid-sixties, de Sade, *My Secret Life*, and in 1965, *The Story of O*, a translation from the French originally written in 1954, Barney kept bringing out a steady flow of lesser erotic works, bearing such tempting titles, for example, as *Harriet Marwood, Governess; The Lustful Turk*; and *Suburban Souls: The Erotic Psychology of a Man and a Maid*. Barney found most of his material in a cache of Victorian and Edwardian pornography in two antiquarian bookshops—the New York Bookstore in Manhattan and J. B. Rund in Brooklyn—as well as in the collection of his sexologist friends, the Kronhausens. For the rest, he commissioned a number of knockoffs of authentic Victorian porn produced by indigent authors eager to collect a salary for four or five weeks' toil. No one much liked them among the staff at Grove, but it was Barney's call, and they did indeed sell.

Barney had no trouble with being identified in the popular mind as a smut merchant. It was part of a perverse satisfaction he took in offending middle-class decorum. A 1969 article in the *Saturday Evening Post* entitled "How to Publish 'Dirty Books' for Fun and Profit," was illustrated with an image of Barney crawling out from underneath a manhole cover. Not a conventionally attractive pose, but Barney liked the idea of (literally) coming out of the underground to besmirch accepted notions of appropriate behavior. He took seriously his role as cultural liberator, delighted when profit could also accompany the liberation.

Barney's commitment to the pleasures of the erotic life went well beyond publishing books extolling the varieties of satisfactions available to the adventurous. His own prolific sexual escapades became the stuff of legend, the source of admiration and envy among his male companions familiar with his alleged nocturnal practices. A "serial womanizer" in his younger days, according to Joe Bianco, a lawyer and close friend, who accompanied Barney on many of his escapades. He noted that women thought him so special that they were reluctant to leave him no matter how badly he treated them. Maurice Girodias, his French publishing alter-ego, who shared many of his aesthetic and sexual appetites, declared that "Barney was always preoccupied with women, and drifted endlessly from . . . one affair to the next, all the while devoting his nights to the most depraved adventures. It wasn't enough for him to cheat on a girlfriend, he wanted to make sure she knew about it."

Following his divorce from Loly in 1957, Barney remained single, but hardly solitary, until 1965, when, at forty-three, he married eighteen-year-old Cristina Agnini, an aspiring dancer whose sister, Luisa, had served as Peter's babysitter. Barney presented a lot to handle for anyone, especially an eighteen-year-old (whom he had met when she was sixteen). But Cristina had grown up in a feisty Italian family where children learned early to negotiate parental and sibling conflict. She received her share of abuse from Barney but returned plenty of her own. Not particularly interested in books, she enjoyed the glamour of the book business that Barney brought to her and the socially active life they lived together. The relationship produced two children, Tansey (1967) and Beckett (1969), and lasted until 1979, when Cristina walked out on him for an affair with a plastic surgeon. Barney was inconsolable at being deserted, swallowing a sufficient number of sleeping pills to require a trip to St. Vincent's Hospital emergency room. When he recovered, he expressed his unhappiness in a less self-destructive mode, tracking down the location of the doctor's car and pouring paint on it. As many of his friends observed, Barney had the capacity, when angry or frustrated, to act like a petulant child.

In 1976, a blond Smith graduate with a master's degree in International Affairs from Columbia University answered an ad in the *Village Voice* for a position as editorial assistant at Grove Press. She could hardly type and had no publishing experience. Predictably, the interviewer told her she would be perfect and immediately hired her. Lisa Krug came to Grove at about the same time that Barney's union with Cristina had entered the death spiral of bickering and mutual recrimination with which his marriages invariably concluded. As things between them continued to come apart, Barney discovered Lisa. Understanding some of the difficulties Cristina experienced in living and working with Barney, Lisa knew that getting involved with him was probably not a wonderful idea. But the excitement of

life at Grove and Barney's tenaciousness were hard to resist.
After Cristina left him, Barney began a full-time relationship
with Lisa; they were married in 1980.

Barney was by turns compelling and inordinately difficult.
He could be affectionate, supportive, brilliantly entertaining—
and contentious, destructive, even vicious. He understood his
own complex impulses in terms of the contrasting styles of two
tennis champions who endlessly fought each other: the elegant
Swede, Bjorn Borg, with his classical ground strokes and calm,
unflappable presence; and the wild American, Jimmy Connors,
playing his frenetic, spontaneous, uncompromising game. In a
1979 letter to Joan, he admits his attraction to both, even if
he recognizes that while he aspires to the Swede, he is locked
onto the American: "And yes!!! I do wish that I was Bjorn
Borg and could serve an ace to the right court . . . you are
so right about him—that fixed determination, that calm, that
obstinate confidence. Somewhere I also hold a love for that
shit Jimmy Connors—his all-out assault time after time—total
risk, total arrogance—no tomorrow. I like that too." Barney
lived with an unmatched intensity. To be with him was to be
enveloped in his energy. Whether reading manuscripts, gar-
dening in East Hampton, or playing tennis, he never let up.
When Claudia Menza visited him in East Hampton one weekend and revealed that she couldn't really play tennis, Barney
had Cristina drive them a mile away and insisted that Claudia run back to the house with him. With all the nastiness he
could dish out, at the same time he provided a kind of hyper-
existence that became addictive.

Lisa wanted a child. Already with three and pushing sixty, Barney was reluctant, but Lisa prevailed. Chantal was born in 1982. Lisa also prevailed in the mode of birth she sought. Barney strongly opposed natural childbirth, maintaining that women should avoid pointless suffering. Lisa tried to explain that women needed to wrest control of their bodies from the medical establishment, and that she wanted to experience the entire process of birth. Barney thought that argument ridiculous. They disagreed passionately, until one day Lisa overheard Barney on the phone explaining to a friend that it was essential for women to wrest control of their bodies from the medical establishment and experience the process of birth without the intervention of drugs. He later accompanied Lisa to Lamaze natural childbirth classes. At Chantal's birth, he filmed the process of labor and delivery and proudly showed the photographs to everybody at Grove, a display of paternal pride that did not delight Lisa.

5

THE STALKING HORSE

Barney always acknowledged the extraordinary gifts of the three talented editors—Don Allen, Dick Seaver, and Fred Jordan—who contributed significantly to Grove's success. If "The Chief," as Barney was known by some, made all the major decisions himself, he relied on the taste and intelligence of his trusty three to help keep publishing writers who mattered and was not in the least reluctant to recognize their efforts. But there was one man, arguably more critical to Grove's achievements even than the others, whom Barney never mentioned: Anthony Comstock, the mutton-chopped zealot who, in 1873, lobbied hard to impose the Comstock Act on the United States, criminalizing any effort to deliver "obscene, lewd, or lascivious" materials through the US mail. Comstock saw lustful impulses everywhere sapping the moral strength of this country and resolved to resist them with all the energy he could summon. His weapon of choice in this battle would be the Post Office. After President Ulysses S. Grant signed the Comstock Act into law, anybody convicted of using the mail for disseminating sexual matter faced ten years in prison and up to a $10,000 fine. Comstock's enthusiasm for the fight led him to be appointed a special agent of the Post Office, authorized to carry a gun and a badge and even empowered to make arrests by himself. Two months after the bill became law, to aid in his quest to expunge the rot he feared was undermining the country's precious moral purity, he founded the New York Society for the Suppression of Vice (NYSSV), becoming its first president, a post he held until his death in 1915.

The self-proclaimed "weeder in the garden of the Lord" loved his work, glorying in the statistical evidence of his effectiveness: near the end of his career he calculated he had been responsible for more than three thousand convictions totaling some 565 years of jail time, nearly three million pictures burned, twenty-eight thousand pounds of printing plates demolished, 318,336 obscene "rubber articles" confiscated, and fifty tons of books destroyed.

From the time Comstock began his fervent weeding in 1873 to the moment Barney discovered his vocation in 1951, the United States' functional definition of what constituted written obscenity, and therefore not legally entitled to pass through the mail, remained essentially unchanged. American morality was protected by a foreign import, formulated in 1868 by the British Lord Chief Justice, Lord Cockburn, who declared that "the test of obscenity is this, whether the tendency of the matter charged as obscenity is to deprave and corrupt those whose minds are open to such immoral influences and into whose hands a publication of this sort may fall." The Hicklin Rule (the case Lord Cockburn resolved was *Regina v. Hicklin*), as it became known, made its way across the Atlantic Ocean, providing Comstock and his successor at the NYSSV, John Sumner, with the legal means to imprison publishers and booksellers, destroy books, terrorize authors—all in the interests of keeping the American reading public free from pollution. It is what caused Norman Mailer, in his bestselling *The Naked and the Dead* (1948), to have to substitute for "fuck"—a word everyone knows and uses—a sound that no one had ever uttered, "fug"; it is what made Swarthmore freshman Barney Rosset go by train to New York to acquire surreptitiously a copy of *Tropic of Cancer* from the Gotham Book Mart; it is what kept James Joyce's masterpiece, *Ulysses*, from being available in the United States until Judge John Woolsey ruled, in 1933, that it wouldn't corrupt its readers' minds.

With his anti-everything sensibility fully formed when he took over Grove, Barney saw in America a veritable candy store of delicious targets to pursue: racism, capitalism, imperialism, and most tempting of all, the repressive censorship ethos of "Comstockery" that prevented people from reading—and writing—whatever they wanted. Barney always said that from the moment he became a publisher his most urgent personal goal focused on bringing the banned *Tropic of Cancer*, the book that meant so much to him at college, before the American reading public. He knew it would not be easy. People viewed Miller as a species of low-grade pornographer, lacking all literary standing. To try to breach the laws against obscenity by using a writer dismissed as second-rate and without any easily discernible moral or artistic credibility would be to ensure failure. If he were to succeed, he would need a strategy, a stalking horse to open the way for copies of Miller to be obtained above instead of under the counter in American bookstores.

The seeds of a plan were unexpectedly delivered to Barney in 1954 in the form of a letter from Mark Schorer, a well-known literature professor at the University of California in Berkeley, suggesting that Grove consider publishing *Lady Chatterley's Lover*, British novelist D. H. Lawrence's last work, written in 1928. Its erotic content and graphic language eminently qualified it as obscene under the Hicklin definition, guaranteeing that it could never be published in an unexpurgated edition either in Britain or the United States. Although Barney didn't much like it at first—he found it heavy-handed, the sex scenes slightly ridiculous—he immediately saw how it might be used in his long-term campaign to free not just *Tropic of Cancer* from the clutches of the censor but all artistic creation in this country. In Barney's words, "If I could get *Chatterley* through the courts on the strength of D. H. Lawrence's fame and reputation as respected author, then it would just be a matter of time before I could slip Henry Miller and his book through the cracks in the cultural barrier raised like a Berlin Wall between the public and free expression in literature, film, and drama." Unlike Miller, whom Barney knew was seen by most people as a kind of bum, a dissolute type you wouldn't want to invite to your home for dinner, Lawrence enjoyed a distinguished status as a significant artist, an acknowledged master of the modern novel, on a par with Conrad and Joyce. Barney understood that even with Lawrence's generous use of "fuck" and "shit," and his reverential (and at times comical) adulation of the male and female genitalia, it would be far easier to argue in court for *Lady Chatterley* as literature, worthy of First Amendment protection, than it would be to make a similar case for Miller's book. And if he could establish the precedent through Lawrence that the obscenity statute could no longer be used to bar a legitimate novel from the mails, then Barney would already have come close to fashioning a plausible defense for *Tropic of Cancer.*

Barney's commitment to publishing books that would challenge the reactionary obscenity laws of the culture set him apart from his publishing brethren, who were unwilling to take the risks, financial and personal, he enthusiastically accepted. He had enormous contempt in particular for Alfred Knopf, who published an expurgated version of *Lady Chatterley* which, in cleaning up Lawrence's language and sanitizing the sex scenes, drained the novel of all its meaning. "In effect," as Barney trenchantly put it, "Lawrence, a writer of towering importance, had been castrated by his own publisher." And though he liked Bennett Cerf of Random House, he was disappointed by Cerf's failure to grasp the urgency of resisting the ban against publishing a serious book by a serious writer. Responding in June 1954 to news that Barney was making plans to release an unexpurgated *Lady Chatterley*, Cerf expressed his reservations: "I can't think of any good reason for bringing out an unexpurgated version of *Lady Chatterley's Lover* at this date. In my opinion, the book was always a very silly story, far below Lawrence's usual standard, and seemingly deliberately pornographic. . . . I can't help feeling that anybody fighting to do a *Lady Chatterley's Lover* in 1954 is placing more than a little of his bet on getting the sensational publicity from the sale of a dirty book."

But before Barney could publish the book, he had to get the rights to it. Lawrence had written three drafts, and Barney asked Schorer if he would go to New Mexico where Lawrence's widow, Frieda, was living, determine which manuscript was the best one to use, and see if he could get her permission to publish it. Frieda and Schorer got along well, and Frieda wrote to Barney agreeing that Grove should issue the unexpurgated version of the third draft, which was closest to Lawrence's artistic and moral intentions. Unfortunately, after Frieda consented, she died, leaving Lawrence's English agent, Lawrence Pollinger, asserting that he alone owned the rights. For reasons Barney never quite understood (he even speculated at one point that it might be anti-Semitism), Pollinger adamantly refused to sell them to Grove, despite Frieda's wishes. Conversations continued sporadically for about nine months, but finally Barney, fearing that he was getting nowhere, decided to shelve the project temporarily.

But only temporarily, as Barney's implacable nature would never permit him to renounce his intention to publish Lawrence.

Devoting his energies to building Grove, Barney let several years go by before hiring Ephraim London, a high-profile lawyer, to investigate the complicated issue of the ownership of the novel's rights. London had all the proper credentials. He had represented the raunchy comedian Lenny Bruce against obscenity charges and successfully defended Roberto Rossellini's film, *The Miracle*, when it was banned in the early fifties. London offered his opinion that the book was out of copyright in the United States and that, in any case, Pollinger had no control over the unexpurgated version that Barney was pursuing. With that, Barney decided in March of 1959 to go ahead with publication. He would ship books across the country by truck.

The next step involved initiating a controlled confrontation with the Post Office to raise the legal issues Barney and London thought they could ultimately win. It required getting some copies of the novel mailed to the United States from abroad so they would be interdicted as obscene matter by Customs. Once they were confiscated, Grove would bring suit against the Post Office, which maintains its own special court, with a member of the department serving as judge. Barney knew Grove would lose the case here, but it would then be in a position to file an appeal in Federal Court, which London felt confident would rule in Grove's favor.

Barney wrote to Joan Landis, a former Grove intern now living in Paris, asking her to mail four copies to him, and then alerted the New York Customs Office that banned material would shortly be delivered to this country. As the books never showed up, he assumed they had been seized, though he failed to receive a response from the three letters he wrote to the Customs officials informing them that the books were en route. Anxious to get started in his legal battle, he telegrammed Landis to airmail another copy, which he promptly took to the New York office to demonstrate that the offensive volume had made its way to him through the US mail. The New York officials were reluctant to make a decision and sent a copy to Washington, to a little known department—the Collector of Restricted Merchandise—for its judicial determination. Finally, Barney was informed by Irving Fishman, deputy collector for restricted merchandise division, that they had impounded all five copies. On April 30, in language that would have made Anthony Comstock's chest swell with pride, New York Postmaster General Robert Christenberry pronounced the book nonmailable: the story of Connie Chatterley leaving her husband, who had been rendered paralyzed and impotent by World War I, and finding sensual gratification and life-giving vitality with their lower-class gamekeeper, Oliver Mellors, was "obscene, lewd, lascivious, indecent, and filthy in content and character. The dominant effect of the book appeals to prurient interest." (Barney later remarked that he discovered in publishing *Lady Chatterley* that "prurient" meant "having an itch.")

The stage was now set for the hearing within the Post Office Department.

Before the hearing commenced, however, an unexpected problem arose. Barney, who never appreciated having his judgment questioned, got into an argument about strategy with

London, a man who felt the same way about his own judgment. As Barney commented, "He thought he was Abraham Lincoln. He wasn't. No one told him." In front of several people, including Mark Schorer and Harry T. Moore, Lawrence's biographer, London imperiously announced they were going to do things his way. That was all Barney needed to hear. He fired him on the spot. "Right there, with the other people there, because I felt so insulted, I remember that I felt, 'I've got to save face if nothing else. I cannot let the man do this.' That was the end."

Barney now had an impending case and no lawyer. But at least his impulsive nature had not deserted him. He knew two lawyers in East Hampton and called them both. The first was not in. The second was Charles Rembar, Norman Mailer's cousin, with whom Barney had played tennis and softball. Barney asked him if he would like to try a case. Despite the fact that he had little time to prepare and had actually never litigated one before, Rembar agreed, and on May 14, 1959, Barney and Rembar went before judicial officer Charles D. Ablard of the United States Post Office. Rembar was assisted by lawyers from the Reader's Subscription Club, who had purchased book club rights from Barney and whose circulars describing the book had also been banned from the mails.

Barney sought to win the case, not by claiming that the Post Office had no constitutional authority to confiscate the books but on the more resonant cultural grounds that like any other work of serious fiction, *Lady Chatterley* was entitled to First Amendment protection. Barney and Rembar didn't want simply to defeat the Post Office on technical grounds, they wanted to make the argument that Grove could legally publish *Lady Chatterley* and in the process diminish the reach of the anti-obscenity laws in general. It was an original approach and not without risk. As Rembar noted, "From Barney's point of view it took considerable courage, because you take a novel legal position that hasn't been tested and you can lose. If you lose, the lawyer's lost a case, but the client can face criminal prosecution."

To defend its literary merit, Barney had amassed testimony from numerous literary critics, intellectuals, and public figures—Professor Mark Schorer; Jacques Barzun, dean of Faculties of Columbia University; Harvey Breit, an editor at the *New York Times Book Review*; and Archibald Macleish, poet and former Librarian of Congress, among others—insisting not only on the book's moral qualities but on its importance for the culture as a whole. Rembar knew that expert opinions of the sort Barney had solicited would have no effect on the hearing, but he wanted to include them so they would be part of the record for the appeal. Rembar also bolstered Grove's case with three witnesses: Barney himself and two literary critics, the venerable Malcolm Cowley and Alfred Kazin.

Rembar began with Barney, questioning him about the history of Grove, the acclaimed authors he had already published and the responsible and dignified way in which he had advertised *Lady Chatterley*, in an effort to establish that Grove was a prestigious company distributing quality literature, not a fly-by-night operation committed to making money off smut.

Barney spoke eloquently about his motives in publishing the book:

> I consider *Lady Chatterley's Lover* to be a great book and a significant part of the heritage of the English-speaking people. As a publisher in a free marketplace, I am also looking for stimulating, challenging, possibly profitable opportunities to publish good books. I stand by this book and every other book that we have brought out. . . .
>
> It occurred to me, and I am sure it occurred to many other publishers, that since 1928 the emotional maturity of the American people has undergone a great change. . . . It occurred to me that it would be incomprehensible if this book were published today that the public would be shocked, offended or would raise any outcry against it; but rather they would welcome it as the republishing, the bringing back to life, of one of our great masterpieces, and therefore I went ahead and published it. Thus far, all of my anticipated feelings have been rewarded with what I expected to happen as having happened, with the exception of this hearing.

Cowley and Kazin defended the book's explicit sexual language and its high artistic purpose. Cowley made a particularly compelling impression with his cherubic complexion, attractive head of white hair, and dignified mustache. As he watched Cowley's cross-examination, Rembar wondered how anyone could find a book obscene that was being defended by such an elegant, decent, obviously moral witness. And Barney noted that Cowley's hearing aid both made him appear fragile and thoughtful while permitting him not to answer certain questions and to deliver pithy lectures instead.

But all the documentation, the convincing testimony of the witnesses, Barney's integrity, and Rembar's incisive arguments came to naught—as Rembar had expected. On May 15, the day following the trial, Ablard declared that he could not render a decision, either on the merits of the case or on Grove's application to suspend the mailing ban while the case was still pending. He referred both matters to Postmaster General Summerfield in Washington. Rembar immediately asked Summerfield to remove the ban while considering his ruling. When Summerfield failed to answer, Grove decided instead to sue New York Postmaster Christenberry—in a sense an innocent bystander, although the man who after all had originally seized the books—asking that he declare them not obscene and forward them through the mails. The day after the suit was filed, on June 10, Summerfield issued his judgment. To no one's surprise, he concluded:

> The contemporary community standards are not such that this book should be allowed to be transmitted in the mails.
>
> The book is replete with descriptions in minute detail of sexual acts engaged in or discussed by the book's principal characters. These descriptions utilize filthy, offensive and degrading words and terms. Any literary merit the book may have is far outweighed by the pornographic and smutty passages and words, so that the book, taken as a whole, is an obscene and filthy work.

The case against Christenberry, with all the evidence that Rembar had included as part of the record, now went to Federal Appeals Court on June 30, to be heard by Frederick van Pelt Bryan, a tough-minded, intellectual judge whose undergraduate curriculum at Columbia College had included immersion in the great books of the Western tradition. Bryan's background and literary intelligence made him the perfect person to listen to Grove's argument about *Lady Chatterley* being a genuine work of art deserving of First Amendment protection. Rembar's tactic was not to assault the legitimacy of the Comstock Act, recognizing as he did that only two years earlier the Supreme Court, in a landmark decision, *Roth v. the United States*, had affirmed the constitutionality of anti-obscenity laws. By so doing, the Court upheld the conviction of Samuel Roth, a New York publisher who had been found guilty of sending an obscene quarterly, *American Aphrodite*, and circulars advertising it, through the mails. Roth, it should be noted, to illustrate the personal risk Barney took in pursuing his case, had been sentenced to five years in prison and a $5,000 fine. As Rembar observed, Barney had something to lose besides an argument. Rather than suggesting that the Court didn't quite get it right at the time—a questionable way to proceed in the best of circumstances—Rembar sought to demonstrate that the laws simply didn't apply to Lawrence's novel.

In finding against Roth, 6-3, the Court would seem to have struck a blow in favor of censorship, but in fact the majority opinion, written by Justice William Brennan, did just the opposite. While endorsing previous Supreme Court rulings that the

US mails could not be used to transport obscene materials, Brennan subtly changed the understanding of what constituted obscenity by stating "that the reason that obscenity was excluded from constitutional protection was not that it had only 'slight value as a step to truth,' but that it did not communicate 'ideas having even the slightest redeeming social importance.'" *American Aphrodite*, in short, was held to be obscene because of its demonstrable and sole purpose to sell copies by appealing to prurient interests. It was otherwise entirely worthless. Although it would take five years (until the Court took on the *Tropic of Cancer* case) for the Brennan opinion to flower into an explicit ruling that would definitively modify the constitutional definition of obscenity, the Roth decision opened the crack in the wall of censorship. And Rembar saw it immediately. If obscenity was limited to that which had no redeeming value whatsoever, then presumably a work that had even the faintest trace of value—social, moral, artistic, psychological, or more or less anything else—came under the embrace of the First Amendment and could not be proscribed. No amount of dirty words, graphic sex scenes, or prurient appeal could affect its constitutionally protected status.

Rembar did not share Barney's absolutist view on the evils of censorship. He could see, as Barney could not, some boundaries that society could legitimately erect for its own protection. He could even understand why well-meaning people could object to the language and sexual descriptions of *Lady Chatterley*. Rembar suggested in his 1968 book, *The End of Obscenity* (a title Barney hated because he felt society's impulses to impinge upon creative freedom would never entirely disappear), that if a referendum had been held in 1959 about whether to publish *Lady Chatterley*, the vote would have been roughly nine-to-one against. But at the same time, he felt that regardless of what he imagined society's majority opinion to be, the novel's moral passion in trying to wrest the possibility of vital, gratifying life from the sterility of Britain's class-ridden society obviously excluded it, through the Roth opinion, from any legal notion of obscenity.

On July 21, Judge Bryan issued his ruling. In spite of the government's position that determinations of the Post Office Department are presumptively correct and should not be upset by the courts unless clearly wrong, Bryan pronounced the book not to be obscene but to fall within the protective authority of the First Amendment. He commented on the seriousness of Grove Press, the tasteful nature of its advertising, the stellar literary reputation of Lawrence, the distinction of the witnesses for the plaintiff and their convincing testimony, and the unanimous critical approval of newspapers across the country, which looked with alarm at the possibility of banning the book. Furthermore, he pointed out that, as Brennan wrote in his Roth opinion, sex and obscenity are not synonymous, and the "portrayal of sex, e.g. in art, literature and scientific works, is not in itself sufficient reason to deny material the constitutional protection of freedom of speech and the press."

Bryan's pronouncement that the "book is almost as much a polemic as a novel," makes clear his conviction that its dominant effect could not possibly be an appeal to prurient interest—an essential feature if it were to be found obscene: "The decision of the Postmaster General that it is obscene and therefore non-mailable is contrary to law and clearly erroneous." Moving into high rhetorical gear in the conclusion of his opinion, Bryan comes close to echoing Barney's own insistence about the importance to society's health of artistic creation unencumbered by censorship: "It is essential to the maintenance of a free society that the severest restrictions be placed upon restraints which may tend to prevent the dissemination of ideas. It matters not whether such ideas be expressed in political pamphlets or works of political, economic or social theory or criticism, or through artistic media. All such expressions must be freely available."

The government appealed, but since the appeals court was on vacation, the case could not be heard until the fall. The three-judge panel met in December; on July 21, 1960, they issued their unanimous opinion: the appeal was denied. The judges firmly rejected the government's argument that the wholesale use of offensive four-letter words and the immoral trajectory of the narrative in which marital promiscuity is rewarded are clear evidence of the novel's obscenity. The court recognized both that words taken out of context cannot be used to define the quality of a novel and that, as Brennan had declared in the Roth opinion, writers are constitutionally permitted to advocate all manner of ideas—"unorthodox ideas, controversial ideas, even ideas hateful to the prevailing climate of opinion."

There was some talk of the Post Office wanting to take the case to the Supreme Court, but the Solicitor General, who determines such matters, decided two defeats were enough. The government gave up: Barney had triumphed. Barney's victory did not generate a vast financial windfall, as many thought. Grove sold fifty or sixty thousand hardcover copies—not a negligible number, to be sure, but also not enormous—though the paperback market, which probably sold several million more, was flooded with inexpensive copies from New American Library, Pocket Books, and Pyramid Books, all of whom waited to see how the trial would turn out before rushing into the copyright void with their editions. Money, however, was never exactly the point at Grove and certainly not here. Barney invariably employed military metaphors in describing his response to censorship: he was "laying siege," "embarking on a legal and cultural trench war," "firing fusillades," "serving as a foot soldier in the struggle" with his "comrades in arms," Dick Seaver and Fred Jordan, and the like. With *Lady Chatterley's Lover*, Barney had fought and won his first engagement. But the major campaign, costly and difficult, lay ahead: *Tropic of Cancer*.

6

ADVENTURES WITH THE HOODED COBRA

"This is not a book. This is libel, slander, defamation of character," *Tropic of Cancer*'s narrator declares at the outset. "This is not a book, in the ordinary sense of the word. No, this is a prolonged insult, a gob of spit in the face of art, a kick in the pants to God, Man, Destiny, Time, Love, Beauty . . . what you will. I am going to sing for you, a little off-key perhaps, but I will sing. I will sing while you croak. I will dance over your dirty corpse." With its provocative sexuality and self-indulgent, filthy language, it represented precisely the kind of project that sheriffs, police chiefs, and assorted other guardians of the public morality lived to prosecute. In ruling the novel obscene, Pennsylvania Supreme Court Justice Michael Musmanno echoed the narrator's own description of it: "*Tropic of Cancer* is not a book. It is a cesspool, an open sewer, a pit of putrefaction, a slimy gathering of all that is rotten in the debris of human depravity." The capacity to inspire such vitriol makes it no surprise that Miller's novel proved to be the most litigated work in the history of American literature.

And no surprise either that Barney risked his personal financial resources and the fiscal health of Grove Press to publish it. He loved it from the time he first read it at Swarthmore, less for the frank, wonderfully vulgar treatment of sexual behavior (which he claimed not really to have noticed) than because he thought it "truly and beautifully anti-conformity." It spoke to Barney's radical nature, his need, despite his wealth, to avoid the psychic traps of a bourgeois existence. The narrator's loss of his first love, Mona, and the despair it engendered also reminded Barney of his own grief over the end of his relationship with Nancy Ashenhurst, followed by the traumatic discovery that she married his good friend Haskell Wexler.

But before he could bring out an American edition of *Tropic of Cancer*, he had to get Miller's consent—not an easy task. The book had originally appeared in 1934 in Paris, issued by Obelisk Press, Jack Kahane's English-language publishing house. Kahane, a British writer-entrepreneur who settled in Paris in the late twenties, made his living by producing some good and a lot of smutty books. But even Kahane had his doubts about *Cancer*. He agreed to publish it only after obtaining a commitment from the writer Anais Nin, Miller's lover and financial supporter, to cover any losses he might incur with it. The novel's shocking contents, of course, guaranteed it would immediately be banned in Britain and the United States.

Barney as a senior at the Parker School, enjoying the good life with his elegant parents.

Always a natty dresser, even at four.

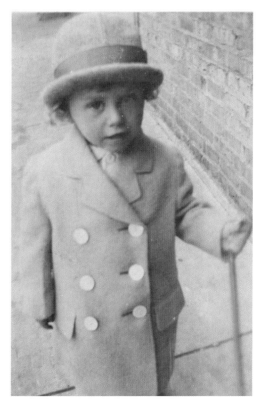

Nancy Ashenhurst, displaying the seductiveness Barney found irresistible at the Parker School.

Second Lieutenant Rosset admiring Gale Barsh before his father intervened to keep him from marrying her.

oan Mitchell in her studio, circa 1948. *Photograph by Barney Rosset, courtesy of the Joan Mitchell Foundation*

Catholic tombstone on the grave of Barney's Jewish father, a man who according to Barney was "hooked on priests."

Barney and Loly (*left*) on their wedding day, August 14, 1953, with John Gruen and Jane Wilson in front of Grove's first office at 795 Broadway.

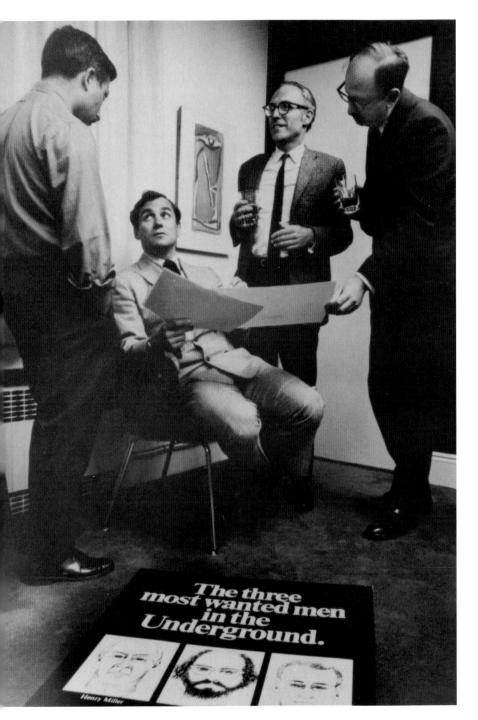

Grove meeting: Nat Sobel, Dick Seaver (*seated*), Barney, and Morrie Goldfischer.

Barney Rosset and Cy Rembar, the attorney who led Grove's legal battle to publish an unexpurgated *Lady Chatterley's Lover*.

David Levine caricature of Barney, 1968. Notice he's typing with women's shoes. © *Matthew and Eve Levine*

arney Rosset and Norman Mailer, late 1960s.

arney Rosset and John Rechy.

This page and opposite: Views of the Chareau Quonset House in East Hampton, where Barney lived from 1952 to 1980.

Barney and his friend, filmmaker Haskell Wexler, 1960.

Trim Barney with his surfboard in East Hampton.

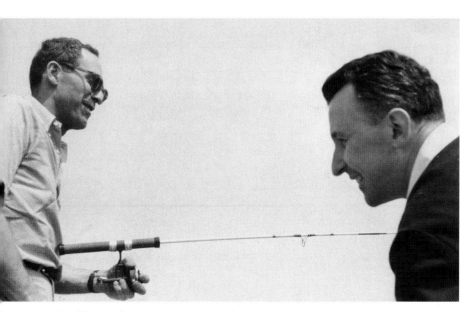

Barney and publisher-friend Maurice Girodias in East Hampton, 1960.

Barney Rosset and
Marguerite Duras, 1967.

Barney relaxing in front of his books, glass of wine in hand. © *Elena Seibert*

Barney's "portrait" of Joan Mitchell, 1989.

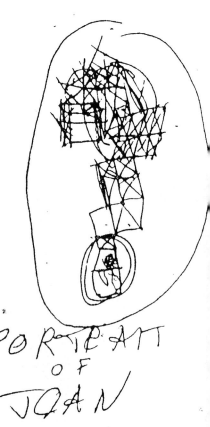

arney's photograph of Samuel Beckett and Lisa Rosset in Paris, 1985. © *Lisa Krug.*
ll rights reserved.

Jobel Prize–winning Japanese novelist Kenzaburo Oe and his beloved "Huckleberry
inn" publisher in Princeton, 1991.

Barney Rosset and George Plimpton.

Ann Getty and Lord Weidenfeld, "the cigar-chomping hippopotamus," in 1985, the year they bought Grove from Barney. © *Arne Svenson*

Barney and Astrid at the French embassy in New York on November 8, 1999, when he was named Commandeur de l'Ordre des Arts et Lettres by the French minister of culture.

Barney playing the game he loved in his loft.

Barney reaching the hard-to-get high places on his loft wall with a paintbrush affixe
to a pool cue and by ascending a stepladder.

Kahane died in 1939, at the outbreak of the war. His son, Maurice Girodias (he adopted his mother's maiden name to avoid Nazi persecution), who at sixteen drew the original cover design for Miller's book, took the firm over, eventually changing its name to Olympia Press. When the war ended, *Tropic of Cancer* rapidly became the smuggled book of choice in the United States, initially brought back by returning GIs, and later, hordes of tourists. In 1948, Ernest Besig thought perhaps the country was mature enough to get beyond the surreptitious confrontation with Miller and tried to import *Cancer* openly through San Francisco customs. Federal judge Louis Godman prevented him, citing the necessity to uphold "the dignity of the human person and the stability of the family unit, which are the cornerstones of our system of society." James Laughlin, the wealthy young owner of New Directions ("Nude Erections," according to the poet Ezra Pound), had earlier purchased the American rights to all of Miller's work but was unwilling to involve himself in the tribulations of publishing the prohibited *Cancer*. So when Barney began negotiating with Miller in 1959, the homegrown Brooklyn boy had for nearly twenty-five years been living the curious existence of enjoying a flourishing international literary reputation while his most famous and best book remained unavailable in the country of his birth.

Miller was by no means entirely unhappy with this odd fact. Although he resented the loss of readership caused by having no legal US sales, for a variety of reasons he was reluctant to give in to Barney's importunings. He had finally reached a point in life where he felt he had enough money to do what he wanted; additional profit would be merely superfluous. With American sales would come publicity and a celebrity status, both of which would interfere with the privacy he sought. And even if Miller appreciated that Barney had beaten down the censors with *Lady Chatterley*, he feared the personal turmoil that would result from a protracted legal battle over *Cancer*. Above all, he had become comfortable with his role as literary outlaw. He liked the notion of his books being smuggled in and then sold, when they could be found, at high prices. He dreaded the thought of becoming a respectable author, included on university reading lists.

Encouraged by Girodias, who was eager to see an American edition of *Cancer*, Barney began writing to Miller, explaining how the country had moved ahead since the *Lady Chatterley* case, and he had no reason to worry about a moral backlash should the book be published. Newspapers and book critics were certainly on his side. Any court battles, he emphasized to Miller, would surely be won by Grove. Miller remained unconvinced, however; he insisted that the decisions to permit *Ulysses* and *Chatterley* into the United States were exceptional, not evidence of a national growth away from repressive Puritanism. At this stage in his life—he was sixty-eight—he didn't want to struggle with police and judges. Miller's resistance could hardly be expected to put Barney off, and he continued to argue for the ease and plausibility of publishing *Cancer* in America, assurances, it turned out, that were rather far from the truth. Finally, in the spring of 1959, Barney decided to make an appeal in person. He flew to California, ascending to Miller's aerie on top of a mountain in Big Sur, with its couch on the lawn overlooking a cliff where Miller liked to receive visitors—and which gave Barney vertigo. In preparation for his visit, Barney had spoken to Miller's wife, Eve. She cautioned him that while she agreed that the book should be published by Grove, as Miller always opposed whatever position she took, she would have to pretend to be against the idea. But Barney should know she was for it.

The meeting proved both unpleasant and unproductive. Barney liked the book but not the author, finding him cold, arrogant, vaguely hostile, and perhaps most damning, lacking in courage. He thought of Miller, whose long face and heavily lidded eyes reminded him of the venomous snake, as "the hooded cobra." Barney made his case; Eve strategically disagreed, and Miller adamantly refused to consider an American edition. As Barney later pointed out, his grand strategy to bring *Tropic* to America "ran into an incredible roadblock: an author by the name of Henry Miller. Quite simply, he didn't want his book published."

Barney drove down from Miller's mountain refuge, disappointed but not defeated. No simple rejection could stop Barney. He continued to write to Miller, warning him about the threat of piracy if he didn't sign with an American publisher, namely Grove; dangling before him substantial amounts of money against royalties if he did. Miller, however, could not be moved. "What I have written cannot be nullified; my works will continue to be circulated in one way or another until they have reached their natural end. The very fact that my books are obtained only with difficulty enhances the prospect of their furtherance. Why go through the torture and mockery of a sensational trial to make them available to any- and everyone? Of what value to me, these additional readers? All that I could hope to acquire thus would be more fame and more money."

Miller's "no" stayed an unbudging "no" until, without any explanation, it suddenly became a "yes." The moment occurred several months after Barney's Big Sur visit. Barney got a telegram from Henry Rowohlt, Miller's German publisher, and Girodias, both of whom were in Hamburg with Miller, announcing that he had changed his mind and that Barney should come immediately. Several days later, Barney arrived in Germany, found Miller in good spirits with a new girlfriend, played ping-pong with him (Barney was an avid player), and with the enthusiastic support of Girodias and Rowohlt, turned him into a Grove author. Following Girodias's suggestion that Barney pay him well, Grove doled out a $50,000 advance—an extremely large sum for the company. Additionally, Barney guaranteed to take care of any legal expenses that might accrue and to keep Miller free from exhausting court appearances. Laughlin, grateful at being delivered from potential confrontations with the law, quickly ceded the rights to *Cancer* (as well as those for *Tropic of Capricorn*) to Grove. Everybody was satisfied, particularly Barney. On April 25, 1961, Grove issued a press release announcing the novel's acquisition; two months later, on June 24, Barney fulfilled his ambition by publishing the book in the United States to strongly positive reviews.

But signing Miller and publishing his novel only marked the start, not the end, of Barney's struggle to give Americans legal access to *Tropic of Cancer*. Unlike the bureaucrats who prosecuted *Lady Chatterley*, opponents of Miller's novel were neither custom officials nor postmasters. The government had learned a painful lesson when Judge Bryan ruled Lawrence's novel not obscene and therefore qualified for constitutional protection. Although the Post Office and customs were eager to enter the obscenity fray again, the Justice Department, which determines participation in these matters, felt the likelihood of winning was extremely slim, opting not to pursue a second case that could—and probably would—end in another humiliating defeat. But *Tropic of Cancer* remained a formidably offensive work, disturbing to all manner of respectable citizens. If the government would no longer be a plaintiff in an action against the book, there were still everyday, hardworking people offended by Miller's moral squalor who were intent on cleansing the filth from libraries, bookstores, and newsstands. Representatives from the Citizens for Decent Literature, an anti-pornographic organization founded in 1958, urged decent-thinking men and women to protest. National book chains were coerced into not carrying it: Doubleday, Scribner's, Brentano's as well as others complied. *Time* magazine called it "a very dirty book indeed," one of those bestsellers "sewer-written by dirty-fingered authors for dirty-minded readers." Without the involvement of the federal judiciary, no central authority existed that could prevent local officials from bringing suit to stop the purchase of the book. And since the police and the DAs were feeling political pressure from national pro-censorship forces, a torrent of prosecutions across the country rained down on those trying to distribute it.

Barney's commitment to defend the First Amendment regardless of the consequences then inspired him to do what no other American publisher would have had the courage—or the divine craziness—to do: underwrite all the expenses, legal and otherwise, of booksellers facing criminal charges for trying to sell the banned volume. Over the next several years, sixty separate cases in twenty-one states were brought against bookstore and newsstand owners and clerks accused of violating local obscenity ordinances. Barney organized defense teams in every instance, absorbing all the costs. His willingness to put his money where his constitutional principles lay marked him as unique in the history of American publishing.

Barney retained Charles Rembar again as his lead counsel, though Rembar was himself able to handle only two of the sixty cases. For the rest, he outlined a general strategy, drawing on his successful experience in applying Justice Brennan's analysis in the Roth opinion to Lawrence, arguing that any trace of social or literary value in a work of art effectively placed it within First Amendment protection. In Rembar's words, at the start of his brief, "It is submitted that this book, being a recognized work of literature, cannot be found to be worthless, and that therefore its publication and sale may not, under the Constitution, be suppressed or impeded." Only utter trash, in short, can be prohibited.

Sometimes it worked and sometimes it didn't, depending on the particular moral ferocity of the local judges, attorneys general, and DAs who were involved and the skill of the defense attorneys. From Amarillo, Texas, to Massachusetts, books were seized and wholesalers cowed. Although there were numerous arrests, there didn't have to be: police intimidation was sufficient to have copies removed from stores throughout the United States.

Anthony Lewis reported in the *New York Times* in January 1962 that it was impossible to buy the book in many major cities of the country, for example, in Los Angeles, Chicago, Philadelphia, Cleveland, Atlanta, Miami, Dallas, Houston, Seattle, Hartford, Wilmington, Indianapolis, Des Moines, St. Louis, Trenton, Buffalo, Phoenix, Oklahoma City, and Birmingham.

Litigation reached six state supreme courts, three—Wisconsin, California, and Massachusetts—finding for the book, and three—New York, Illinois, and Florida, against. The Illinois proceeding in January of 1962 was Barney's favorite, the only trial in which he served as a witness. Grove, in this case, was acting as the plaintiff, suing the Chicago police for illegally interfering in the sale of the book. Grove's prominent lawyer, Elmer Gertz, put on the stand as the first witness Professor Richard Ellmann, a distinguished literature professor and acknowledged James Joyce authority. Ellmann argued eloquently for the novel's power and significance, making clear it could in no way be understood as obscene. Ellmann remained imperturbable in the face of the cross-examination's effort to rattle him. When asked about "the method of masturbation employed by one of the characters where he cores out the center of the apple and smears it with cold cream and uses it in that fashion," Ellmann was not fazed in the least: "I should say it was slightly disgusting but that it's an essential element in the disgusting picture of the *Tropic of Cancer* which is a diseased civilization. You must represent disease as disease." Gertz followed Ellmann's expert testimony with Barney, who described Grove's publishing history, the role it played in providing texts for hundreds of the best colleges and universities in the land, the care it took in avoiding any salacious appeal in its advertising. As to whether Barney would be happy to have his own children read the book, a question raised by the lawyers for the police, he replied, "I would imagine that I would be perfectly content to have my child read this book whenever he or she wished to do so. [As was indeed the case in the Rosset house.] If another parent felt differently, I wouldn't argue with him." It was better to have even the wrong people read a book than to have nobody read it, he suggested.

The most gratifying moment in Barney's testimony occurred during the cross-examination, when the defense accused Barney of having no real appreciation or knowledge of Miller but merely wanting to make money off him by publishing his dirty book. Although Barney hadn't necessarily anticipated this particular challenge, he had come prepared. He pulled out of his pocket his Swarthmore English paper, "Henry Miller Versus Our Way of Life," and began reading out loud from the witness box. As Barney later commented with amusement, the B- college paper had the power of an A+ essay in the Chicago courtroom. The DA was appropriately flummoxed; the cross-examination came to an immediate halt and Barney was dismissed, not to be called back.

The case was heard before Judge Samuel Epstein, an old friend of Barney's father, a fact of which Barney was initially unaware. After the first day, a young man introduced himself to Barney as Judge Epstein's son. He confided to Barney that his father had suggested that if Grove slightly altered its legal strategy, chances of its winning would be considerably enhanced. Barney passed the information on to Gertz, who adjusted his tactics accordingly. Barnet Sr.'s friendship with the judge had provided Barney with a precious gift, posthumous though it was, which made Barney feel he could still count on his father for help.

Epstein announced his decision on February 21, 1962. Although he personally found the book distasteful, he objected even more to all efforts to shape the thinking of mature citizens:

> Let the parents control the reading matter of their children; let the tastes of the readers determine what they may or may not read; let not the government or the courts dictate the reading matter of a free people.
>
> The constitutional right to freedom of speech and press should be jealously guarded by the courts. As a corollary to the freedom of speech and press, there is also the freedom to read. The right to free utterances becomes a useless privilege when the freedom to read is restricted or denied.

Epstein's opinion was just one of many, and was eventually overturned by the Illinois Supreme Court, but it sounded a magnificent note of freedom. It convinced Barney that ultimately the battle against oppression would be won. "The right to read" declaration became the clarion call of those resisting censorship of any sort. It soon gathered 198 signatures of writers, critics, and publishers in support of the decision, and Barney printed Epstein's opinion and their names on the cover and inside two pages of *Evergreen Review* No. 28.

But meanwhile, the brush fires of local banning and the seizure of copies of *Cancer* continued to occur and had to be continually fought. Miller, who stayed far from the action on top of his mountain in Big Sur, left Barney to do all the work. The hooded cobra's major contribution to the cause was to recommend the case be brought before the Supreme Court— in Miller's mind, a simple matter at Barney's disposal. Barney tried to explain the difficulties involved in getting the Court to accept a case. He also sought to get Miller to comprehend these were perilous times for Grove, as they were fighting to stay alive. He later estimated that roughly 90 percent of Grove's energy following publication of the book necessarily focused on defending the company from criminal prosecution.

Miller's immunity from the varied court battles finally came to an end in the fall of 1962 when a Brooklyn grand jury agreed to consider the charge that he, Barney, and Grove Press were guilty of conspiring to produce an obscene work. Miller, whose courage Barney had never regarded as his strongest attribute, still refused to leave California. Barney, on the other hand, always supercharged by moments of risk and crisis, went confidently to the hearing. The DA's inclusion of all three—author, publisher, and press—in a single conspiracy represented the triumph of eagerness to prosecute over lawyerly attention to detail. As Barney pointed out, when the scheme was allegedly being hatched in Brooklyn in 1934, Miller was in Paris, Grove didn't exist, and Barney was a twelve-year-old student in Chicago. These embarrassing blunders notwithstanding, District Attorney Silver opened his case assertively with the slightly stale ploy of the corruption of the innocent, trying to shame Barney by noting that the jurors' children could currently buy the text in an inexpensive paperback edition. But Barney would have none of it: "Well, that's very good," he replied. "And if their children bought that book and read it all the way through, then those parents should be congratulated." Then Silver asked Barney to read aloud a particularly vulgar section of *Tropic*, a passage that police all over the country had used as evidence for the book's obscenity. Unfortunately for Silver, the jury started to laugh, finally causing Silver himself to laugh and the jury to refuse to indict.

With his presentation to the grand jury in shambles, Silver then produced an Information, a charge a DA can bring on his own when unable procure an indictment from the jury. Barney was accused of conspiracy to commit a crime—publishing a lewd book—as well as actually committing it, a misdemeanor carrying a maximum sentence of three years imprisonment. Rembar pleaded not guilty on Barney's behalf, and though Silver wanted a $500 bail, Barney was released on his own recognizance. A warrant for Miller's arrest was later issued by the

Criminal Court, but the Brooklyn DA never made an effort to extradite him from California.

If Judge Epstein's eloquent defense of the right to read encouraged Barney to believe that freedom was on the way to defeating censorship, it did nothing to still the protests of those who objected to the privilege of uncensored reading. Prosecutions and harassments continued throughout 1962 and 1963, with local authorities struggling to keep Miller's subversive energies from corrupting the population. Grove could address the individual disputes, but it couldn't prevent new ones from breaking out or the expenses from mounting. Only the Supreme Court, as Miller had naively but accurately understood, could, with a single ruling, establish a judicial understanding of obscenity that might protect a writer's creative freedom and incidentally end the attacks on Grove. But as Barney had explained to Miller at the time, one did not just "bring" a case before the Supreme Court.

Grove did have at its disposal one method to try to appear before the Court: petitioning for certiorari, a technique to get the Court to listen to an appeal from a state court on the grounds either that a state statute is unconstitutional or the appealing party has been denied a federal constitutional right in the lower court. By 1964, Grove's main lawyers, Rembar and Gertz, had determined to try to end the debilitating legal skirmishing by filing for certiorari in two states, Illinois and Florida. Illinois seemed much more promising, as Grove's Florida lawyers had previously agreed to waive all constitutional issues on their way to initially losing in an intermediate court. Grove was advised that because there were no relevant constitutional questions, there was little chance that the Supreme Court would accept the case. But even as Grove was working out the approach for the Illinois petition, they chose nevertheless to go ahead in Florida.

Whether it was to put a halt to the divisiveness generated by having the highest state courts disagree with each other or end the confusion surrounding clashing lower-court opinions or simply owing to the merciful perception that three years' interminable litigation required some sort of final resolution, the Court, much to everybody's surprise, opted to rule on it. On June 22, 1964, by a vote of 5-4, the Court reversed Florida's lower-court decision that *Tropic of Cancer* was obscene. The five justices offered no specific justification for their decision. Instead, they declared they were reversing for the reasons they had given earlier on that same day when they overturned an Ohio court's decision, in *Jacobellis v. Ohio*, which had found a movie, *The Lovers*, obscene. The majority opinion, written by Justice William Brennan, dealt with the film but included the novel within its legal reasoning. Returning to the issue of value he had tentatively explored in his decision on the Roth case, Brennan explicitly drew his Roth thoughts together into a fully orchestrated pronouncement on how obscenity differs from constitutionally protected speech:

We would reiterate, however, our recognition in Roth that obscenity is excluded from the constitutional protection only because it is "utterly without redeeming social importance," and that "the portrayal of sex, e.g. in art, literature and scientific works, is not itself sufficient reason to deny material the constitutional protection of freedom of speech and press." It follows that material dealing with sex in a manner that advocates ideas . . . or that has literary or scientific or artistic value or any other form of social importance, may not be branded as obscenity and denied the constitutional protection. Nor may the constitutional status of the material be made to turn on a "weighing" of its social importance against its prurient appeal, for a work cannot be proscribed unless it is "utterly" without social importance.

Although it took several months before all legal attempts to interfere with the sales of *Tropic* stopped, Barney had finally succeeded, with a major assist from William Brennan, in changing the rules regarding censorship in America. Unwittingly—and certainly unintentionally—Miller had led Barney to his greatest victory. Old Smut Peddler though he might have been, Barney also deserves to be recognized as the twentieth-century's most intrepid First Amendment warrior.

At the same time that Barney was busy fending off the assaults of the morally outraged on *Tropic of Cancer* in the early sixties, he stashed away in Grove's New York warehouse ten thousand copies of a book that even he knew the country was not yet prepared for. Until he could settle *Tropic's* status as a novel people could buy in their local bookstore, it would be an act of madness to try to publish William Burroughs's *Naked Lunch*, a book, he later claimed, which went "far, far, far beyond *Tropic of Cancer*. This was *Star Wars!*" A mad, surreal pastiche of drug-induced fragments, put together over a period of nine years from notes compiled about the delirium of addiction, bits and pieces of stories, and material from Burroughs's letters to his friends, Beat writers Allen Ginsberg and Jack Kerouac, *Naked Lunch* bears little resemblance to a conventional work of fiction. It lacks any plot, any kind of character development, any easily discernable coherence. For some, reading it is akin to experiencing the chaotic energy of a Jackson Pollock canvas. The novelist Mary McCarthy suggested that encountering the book is like "seeing a neighborhood movie with continuous showings that you can drop into whenever you like."

Burroughs was a wealthy, Harvard-educated junkie who for fifteen years prior to the book's publication had absorbed into his body every conceivable kind of opium product through every conceivable point of entry: "I have smoked junk, eaten it, sniffed it, injected it in vein-skin-muscle, inserted it in rectal suppositories." Prevailed upon by friends Ginsberg, Kerouac, and others to capture his junkie world on paper, Burroughs, based finally in Tangier, had by the mid-fifties accumulated sufficient pages of tattered handwritten manuscript to pass on to Ginsberg for typing and editing. Ginsberg became his unofficial agent, toting the unkempt pile of papers around Europe to different publishers. He twice approached Girodias with what he claimed was a completed version—the first time in 1956—to see if he would consider it for his Olympia Press and was twice refused.

Through Ginsberg's efforts, portions of the book began appearing in small magazines in the United States. When the University of Chicago's literary magazine published a chapter in the fall of 1958, an incensed Chicago gossip columnist raised a furor. The university's provost immediately suspended the next issue, which threatened to include additional material from the novel. The student editors resigned in protest and started their own magazine, *Big Table*, whose initial number predictably contained other Burroughs excerpts. Equally predictably, the Post Office confiscated copies of the first issue in March 1959, on grounds that it was a crime to send obscene material through the mails. A suit promptly brought by the ACLU against the Post Office generated enough controversy about the book (the ACLU eventually won the case in 1960) to cause Girodias to rethink his dislike of its incoherence and violence in the interests of capitalizing on the free publicity; by August, Girodias' English-language Olympia Press had printed five thousand copies in Paris.

Always in need of money, Girodias pondered the sale of American rights to enhance his income, and looking across the ocean, chose Barney, the idiosyncratic American publisher who shared many tastes, literary and otherwise, with him. Barney was of course interested. How could he not be, in a work that Burroughs himself described as "brutal, obscene and disgusting," by turns hilarious and grotesque, featuring necrophilia, excrement-eating, cannibalism, a talking anus, and minutely detailed, vicious acts of rape, all the while excoriating the dishonesty of contemporary society? For Norman Mailer, "One had to enter this terrible borderland of sex, sadism, obscenity and horror and anything else because somehow the conscience of Western man has become altogether muddy in refusing to enter it. . . . That is why I salute Burroughs' work, because he has gone further into it than any other Western writer today."

Clearly Barney's kind of book, violating sexual, political, and ethical boundaries in ways that excited him. French novelist Alain Robbe-Grillet thought that Barney was as attracted to the outrageous side of the man as much as to his book. He pointed out that Barney was fascinated by Burroughs's "William Tell" gesture one drunken night in a Mexican bar in 1951, when Burroughs convinced his wife to place a glass on top of her head so he could exhibit his firm hand in shooting it off. Unfortunately, alcohol had rendered his hand less firm than he thought and the demonstration ended only by showing that a bullet in the head is likely to prove fatal. Mexican authorities treated it as an accident.

Barney termed the book a work of genius and purchased the rights from Girodias in November of 1959. But before he could publish it, he became swept up in the controversy and expense over *Tropic of Cancer*. While he defended the one, it would have been the wrong time for Grove to release another inflammatory volume. As Barney wrote to Girodias two years later, "It would be absolutely suicidal to publish *Naked Lunch* at this moment. . . . We have printed 10,000 copies . . . but we are not going to publish it right now, and furthermore I can make no promise to you as to exactly when we will be able to do so."

Because Girodias's contract with Barney called for him to get one-third of the American royalties, and given the fact that his need for funds had not diminished, he kept badgering Barney to publish, but Barney continued to refuse. By 1962, however, with prospects beginning to brighten for *Tropic of Cancer*, Barney started to reexamine his position. An International Arts Festival at Edinburgh that August, at which Mary McCarthy and Norman Mailer celebrated Burroughs's brilliance, encouraged Barney to think that perhaps the time had come. He consulted with Edward de Grazia, a lawyer who had been involved in some of the *Tropic* litigation. De Grazia assured him that they could, if necessary, win in the courts and should proceed to distribute the ten thousand warehoused volumes, as long as Barney would refrain from offering the indemnification guarantees he had extended to booksellers stocking the Miller novel. Without the financial vulnerabilities he had previously imposed upon himself, Barney, the man of impulse, decided to publish the book he liked, regardless of the consequences. A Grove flyer to bookstores went out on October 30, announcing the impending publication, in Norman Mailer's words, of "an authentic masterpiece . . . a book of great beauty, great difficulty, and maniacally exquisite insight," written, according to Jack Kerouac, by "the greatest satirical writer since Jonathan Swift." *Naked Lunch* became available on November 20. Within a month, it had sold almost eight thousand copies.

The legal harassment that Barney feared never occurred. *Tropic of Cancer's* court victories had softened the censorious opposition, and the country seemed slightly more inclined to recognize the freedom of artists to write however and whatever they wished. With one exception. In 1963, Boston brought criminal charges against Theodore Mavrikos, a bookseller, for selling allegedly obscene materials, namely *Naked Lunch*. De Grazia immediately went to Boston to argue that Massachusetts law, properly understood, required civil action to be instituted against the book, not criminal action against the seller. This was an important step, for only if the book were charged, not the man, would Grove have an opportunity to defend its literary virtues in court. It took nearly a year and a half for the Massachusetts attorney general (later senator) Edward W. Brooke to drop the charges against Mavrikos and file a petition against *Naked Lunch*. Moving for dismissal but knowing he would not get it, de Grazia spent the next months working out with Barney a list of distinguished witnesses prepared to speak about the novel's merits. Like Miller, Burroughs was not interested in appearing in court to defend his own work, but Grove compiled an impressive group of writers, professors, and psychologists, including Professor Norman Holland of MIT, the poet and critic John Ciardi, and writers Allen Ginsberg and Norman Mailer. Despite the eloquent testimony he assembled, de Grazia expected to lose in the lower court; he was not disappointed. On October 8, 1965, Judge Eugene Hudson dismissed the claims that it was a moral book, even, according to Professor Holland, "a religious novel about original sin," instead declaring it "obscene, indecent, and impure," and without any redeeming social or artistic value. And he added that he found its author mentally ill.

Six months later, the case came before a seven-judge appellate court, which took another nine months before reaching a decision. Finally, on July 7, 1966, the court handed down a 5-2 opinion in favor of *Naked Lunch*. Following the logic of the Brennan ruling, in the instances of *Tropic of Cancer* and *The Lovers*, which held that any traces of social importance meant that the work could not be deemed obscene, it asserted that Burroughs's novel dealt with serious issues and consequently was entitled to First Amendment protection. Although dissenting justice Paul Reardon refused to go down without one last vituperative swipe at the horrors unleashed upon the public without the protection of the censor, characterizing the book as "a revolting miasma of unrelieved perversion and disease graphically described . . . it is, in truth, literary sewage," Barney—and America—had won. Book censorship had effectively ended: *Naked Lunch* was the last work of fiction to come before a US court on obscenity charges. Thanks to Barney, in the words of Ted Morgan, Burroughs's biographer, "Americans were finally allowed to read what they wanted."

7

RIDING THE GALES
OF THE SIXTIES

With the appellate court's exoneration of *Naked Lunch*, Barney completed a publishing trifecta (Lawrence, Miller, Burroughs) that moved the country closer to recognizing his ideal of the sacrosanct nature of the First Amendment. No one but Barney was prepared to undertake the struggle; no one but Barney could have prevailed. Whatever else Barney accomplished, he had earned for himself an enduring place in publishing history.

His legacy notwithstanding, Barney still had a business to run, and one that had been badly crippled by the cost of fighting the evils of censorship. When publisher Jason Epstein declared that Barney "had a funny thing about money—he didn't like it"—he was not entirely correct. Barney had nothing against money; he was just not intent on making it or adept at keeping it. While he understood the necessity of businesses to have some, his primary commitment to publishing books he liked tended to relegate bottom-line considerations to annoying afterthought. He preferred to spend his time with books that attracted him rather than with those he thought simply might sell. A philosophy not without its problems. As Claudia Menza said about Barney, "Had he been a better businessman, he might not have been as great a publisher."

Barney attributed some of his achievements to the fact that "I rode the gales of the 60s," which blew in a variety of directions and with different intensities, sweeping out the stability of Norman Rockwell's cozy world and bringing in its place revolutions, the Beatles, assassinations, civil rights demonstrations, the growth of black power, anti-Vietnam protests, student riots, the evolution of the New Left, sexual liberation, and the women's movement. Barney not only rode the gales, he was in part a generator of the winds that transformed American society. Barney's feisty, anti-everything sensibility gave voice to the emerging counterculture that replaced the aspirations for corporate security celebrated in Sloan Wilson's popular 1955 novel (and later film), *Man in the Gray Flannel Suit*. Grove supplied the books that taught university students the blessings of revolution, the pleasures of the body, 1001 ways to beat the draft—which began with groping FBI director J. Edgar Hoover and ended with bringing peace to Vietnam and joy to the universe—and how to make Molotov cocktails.

The "radical anomaly" remained eternally young—some might say adolescent—and understood from the start of his publishing career that an important audience for Grove would be college-age students. To capitalize on this connection and funnel books into the higher education curriculum, Grove devised a school and college catalogue and sent it to colleges and universities across the country. In the spring of 1967, it caught the attention of august British historian J. H. Plumb, who called it, in the *Saturday Review of Literature*, a "tragic comment on contemporary American life" that announced the "moral decadence of capitalistic societies" in a way that would gladden the hearts of the Viet Cong or the Chinese Red Guard or idealistic Soviet teachers. Focusing on nine books out of the catalogue of 250, including the works of Henry Miller, Burroughs, and the Marquis de Sade, Plumb inveighed against the bias toward sex, sodomy, and drug addiction they reveal: "A ridiculous diet for school or college—as dangerous as dynamite for the young." He concluded his diatribe with the dismissive judgment that the catalogue "must be one of the blackest and sickest jokes of our time."

Barney responded a month later with a letter to the editor, referring to the poetry Grove published, its anthologies of world literature, and the distinguished social scientists in the catalogue. If Plumb wants to amuse himself, Barney suggested, "he should try Joe Miller [the apocryphal joke teller] rather than the Grove Press School and College Catalogue."

Without a strict ideology or any kind of calculated marketing strategy, Barney trusted his own instincts and passions (and those of his senior editorial colleagues) to publish writers others were not interested in or had simply overlooked. The unlikely path to Grove's all-time bestseller began with a letter from Canadian psychiatrist Eric Berne suggesting that Barney publish his *Games People Play: The Psychology of Human Relationships*. Grove had previously published Berne's study on transactional analysis, which had sold modestly. Berne accompanied the submission of his manuscript with a recommendation that the initial printing should be one hundred thousand copies. Dick Seaver and Barney, skeptical about the potential audience, decided that five thousand copies would be more appropriate, a number that seemed especially safe when Berne agreed to buy half of those for his own use. Much to everybody's amazement (except obviously Berne's), the book, published in 1964, never stopped selling. It stayed on the *New York Times* bestseller list for two years. When Seaver acknowledged that Berne had been right after all, Barney disagreed, pointing out that Berne had severely underestimated the book's success.

Barney's willingness to take chances by listening to people he trusted led him to an obscure Martinique-born psychiatrist and revolutionary, Frantz Fanon, a staunch supporter of violent Algerian resistance to French colonial rule. Seaver had read the French edition of *The Wretched of the Earth*, which he thought original and important. A three-minute conversation with Dick was all it took to convince Barney of Fanon's significance. Grove published it in 1965 and watched it become a key text for anticolonial sentiment around the world.

Fanon, in turn, led Barney to Malcolm X, the black American Muslim minister whose thinking was strongly influenced by Fanon's writings. When Malcolm was gunned down on February 21, 1965, in the Audubon Ballroom in upper Manhattan by three killers from the Nation of Islam, his autobiographical manuscript was about to be typeset into galleys by Doubleday. Several weeks after the assassination, Barney learned that Nelson Doubleday had decided to cancel publication out of concern for the safety of his company and its employees. Nothing stimulated Barney's appetite for a book more than another publisher's rejection of it. Doubleday's change of mind contributed to Barney's total certainty that Malcolm and Grove were meant for each other. He was right. He quickly obtained the rights from Malcolm's widow, Betty Shabazz, and brought the book out later that year; it instantly became a bestseller and one of the important books of the decade. By August 1968, the paperback edition had sold three-quarters of a million copies.

Barney might have been indifferent to bottom-line concerns, but he was by no means oblivious to the fragility of Grove's fiscal condition. By the early sixties, the slim profits the company actually generated had been seriously eroded by the legal costs associated with the publication of Lawrence, Miller, and Burroughs. The success of Berne and Malcolm X in 1964 and 1965, along with healthy sales of *Last Exit to Brooklyn* (1964), *The Wretched of the Earth* (1965), and *The Story of O* (1965), encouraged Barney to explore taking the company public in an effort to shore up its finances. Early in 1967, Barney asked Dick Seaver how he would feel about the possibility of Grove issuing a public offering of 240,000 shares sometime in the summer. Wall Street was looking favorably at them, and at an initial price of between six and ten dollars, Grove would realize well over a million dollars.

Seaver and the other senior executives were excited not only for the health of the company but for their own personal well-being, as all were slated to receive an option to purchase four thousand shares. The stock opened for trading in July of 1967, listed on the NASDAQ exchange at $7.00. It immediately became a hot issue, with stock analysts significantly overvaluing it, going as high as forty dollars a share. While the editors entertained fantasies of becoming rich as the value continued to rise, Barney unfortunately had neglected to inform them that the "letter stock" they possessed had to be held for a certain period before it could be redeemed. By the time they were entitled to profit, enthusiasm for the shares had waned to the point where they were selling for under a dollar. In the end, neither Grove nor its employees prospered through its transformation into a public company. "A harsh introduction to the vagaries of the stock market," Dick Seaver later commented, "as well as a concrete example of the law of gravity."

From the moment in eighth grade that he first read *Red Star Over China*, Edgar Snow's glowing account of Mao and his Long March, Barney was hooked on the appeal of revolution. Although his dreary affiliation with the Communist party in Chicago while he attended the university revealed just how incompatible they were on vital matters of art, literature, and freedom of expression, Barney never lost his radical sympathies. If Russia could not be a focus for them, there was always Algeria and above all, Cuba. In their guerrilla campaign against Batista's dictatorship, begun in 1959, Fidel Castro and Che Guevara captured the imagination of the man who had always lamented that his youth had kept him from fighting for the republic in the Spanish Civil War. Barney was an ardent supporter of the Cuban revolution from the beginning. He particularly admired the darkly charismatic Che, as much for the romantic aura he created around him as for the military help he gave Castro. Barney saw Che as leading the heroic existence that he had always sought for himself.

At about midnight on March 27, 1968, as he was getting ready to go to bed, Joe Liss, a writer and news correspondent friend of Barney's, got a phone call from him. He was in a Third Avenue bar and wondered whether Joe could join him immediately. Joe said he was in his pajamas, but could certainly dress quickly and get down if it was important. Barney replied that it could wait until the next morning; he simply wanted to talk to Joe about his interest in going to Bolivia to obtain Che Guevara's diaries for Grove. Joe hung up, unsure whether Barney was high or drunk or just having fun. After a sleepless night, Joe called Barney, who assured him he was totally serious and needed his help. Che had been killed in Bolivia in October of 1967, and Barney had learned that portions of his Bolivian diaries might be available for sale if one contacted the right general with the right amount of money. Barney wanted to publish them—badly. As at least one other publisher—McGraw Hill—was also interested, he knew he had to act expeditiously.

Liss was the second man Barney had called about Bolivia. The first, several months earlier, was John Nathan, a friend who had become the English translator of Grove's distinguished Japanese author Kenzaburo Oe. Nathan's wife had just produced their first child, and though he felt considerable hesitance about leaving his son and going off disguised as an American professor in search of a rogue general, he finally capitulated to Barney's insistence. Barney, as Nathan observed, "was wildly excited; next to court battles, this kind of intrigue was his favorite topic."

Nathan's resolve, however, shortly crumbled; a horrifying dream of being struck by a cyanide dart precipitated a withdrawal phone call, much to Barney's displeasure. Writing later to Oe, Barney complained of "John Nathan's cowardly escaping the chance to visit Bolivia." Nathan admitted that his decision was shameful, but it nevertheless pained him to think of his two friends sitting in judgment on him. With Nathan reneging, Barney turned to Liss.

When Liss arrived at the office, he found airline tickets, an itinerary, a cover story (screenwriter from New York and London needing the diaries for research on a film about Che), $8,500 in fifties and hundreds for the purchase, and strict instructions never to try to contact Barney directly but always to communicate—all cables and calls—through Joe's wife, Mildred, in New York. Plans were even made for him to receive a cable from an alleged screen producer at his hotel in Bolivia to authenticate the Che movie-writing project. On

March 29, "707 Liss," as he self-mockingly referred to himself on his secret mission, arrived at his hotel in La Paz.

For the next several weeks, Liss bumbled about La Paz, holding meetings, missing meetings, and pursuing various newspaper reporters, generals, radical priests, and assorted others who had, or who at least claimed to have, some portions of the diary. Selling diary excerpts throughout Bolivia had suddenly become big business, and Liss did his best to find what he could. He kept Barney informed of his progress through phone calls with murky reception to Mildred, some of which he had no doubt were being tapped. At the start of the third week of what was originally intended to be a three-day trip, Liss received a call from Barney, code-named Roger Tansey (Barney's maternal grandfather). When Liss expressed his happy surprise at the clarity of the connection, "Tansey" explained it was because he was actually speaking to him from La Paz, where he had flown with Fred Jordan to assist in the acquisition. Together the three men continued their pursuit, rounding up six pages of diary, some photos of Che, and a book manuscript from two journalists, Gustavo Sanchez and Luis Gonzalez, which Grove later published as *The Great Rebel: Che Guevara in Bolivia*. Barney worried that the Bolivian authorities might try to confiscate Che's papers when they left the country, but the three avoided the difficulty when Jordan simply put the pages in his pocket and no one at the airport asked about them. Liss celebrated his return to New York, happy to escape from the remoteness of Bolivia, where he felt entirely cut off from the world, unable to read an English newspaper for three weeks. He had to learn about the assassination of Martin Luther King (April 4, 1968) from a Dupont salesman selling dynamite in Bolivia who happened to have a shortwave radio.

Evergreen Review No. 51, published in February 1968, contained a special section that commemorated Che's life, featuring excerpts from Che's own *Reminiscences of the Cuban Revolutionary War*, his account of the role he played in helping defeat the Cuban dictator. Barney also included in this issue the emotional farewell speech Castro gave honoring him—"El Che Vive!"—in which he declared that Che's death "will, in the long run, be like a seed, which will give rise to many men determined to imitate him, determined to follow his example." With Paul Davis's haunting image of Che on the cover, wearing his Marxist beret and a Christlike beatific expression on his face, Barney had essentially turned Grove and *Evergreen* into this country's unofficial purveyor of the Cuban revolution. "The spirit of Che," as the cover proclaimed, lived on in *Evergreen*.

It was not an association that everyone necessarily liked. The August issue of *Evergreen Review*, No. 57, came out late in July, with the diary pages that Barney had gathered in Bolivia. At roughly three in the morning of July 26, a pickup truck slowed down outside the University Place office of Grove Press long enough for its occupants to fire a rocket-propelled grenade through the second-floor window of the production department. As no one was there at the time no one was hurt, though the blast did serious damage. After the incident, while walking around the shambles of the office, which was filled with police, Barney noticed a fresh knife wound in the middle of the Paul Davis poster of Che on the wall. In response to the police mumbling something about the attackers being responsible, Barney expressed his amazement that a knife could have been thrown so accurately up two stories from the street. The police remained silent on the issue.

Following the explosion, which took place on the fifteenth anniversary of the start of Castro's revolution, which was celebrated as a national holiday in Cuba, the Associated Press received a phone call announcing that the assault had been mounted by the commandos of the MNCC—Movimiento Nacional de Coalition Cubano—in response to the publication of Che's diary and Grove's support of international communism. The commandos turned out to be Cuban exiles, several of whom were reserve officers in the American Air Force and, according to Barney, had worked for the CIA. They were shortly apprehended, but nothing happened to them: Barney claimed the judge said they were good people, had never done anything wrong before, and dismissed the charges—only nourishing his suspicions of the government's involvement in anti-Grove activities. But whatever one makes of Barney's conspiracy theories, he must have taken some kind of perverse pleasure in seeing the impecunious company he bought from Phelps and Balcomb achieve the distinction of becoming the sole publishing house in American history to have been bombed because of its political commitments. He had come a long way from the days of Crashaw, Melville, and Mrs. Aphra Behn.

A curious footnote to the tumultuous summer of 1968: Almost one month before the bombing, Valerie Solanas, the founder and sole member of SCUM (Society for Cutting Up Men), began hanging around outside Grove's University Place building with an ice pick. A radical feminist writer, Solanas had earlier submitted the SCUM manifesto to Grove, calling for "civic-minded, responsible, thrill-seeking females" to "overthrow the government, eliminate the money system, institute complete automation and destroy the male sex." Solanas had grown impatient with Barney's failure to publish it. Grove employees, aware of her presence, feared that she was planning to kill him. Warned one day as he prepared to go to lunch that she was outside, Barney replied to his informant, "Dear, if I ran away from everybody was who going to kill me with an ice pick or some other thing, I'd never go to lunch at all. I'm going at one o'clock. He ate with impunity. Several days later, however, Solanas, who felt that Andy Warhol had either stolen or lost the play she had sent him, *Up Your Ass*, went to his factory with a revolver she had exchanged for her ice pick and shot him, almost fatally.

One month after the grenade attack, on August 25, Barney set out from his East Hampton home to drive to Chicago, the site of the 1968 Democratic convention. It promised to be a memorable event, with Hubert Humphrey and Gene McCarthy vying to replace Lyndon Johnson and antiwar protestors flocking to the windy city to make the nomination process a referendum on Vietnam. Preparing for trouble, the legendary mayor, Richard J. Daley, and the Chicago police guaranteed it would occur. Barney's friends—such as Haskell Wexler, arriving to make a movie (*Medium Cool*) of the experience, Jean Genet, covering it for *Esquire*, and editor Dick Seaver and Allen Ginsberg, planning to observe and demonstrate—would be there, and Barney had no intention of missing it. Or so he thought. By the time he reached Southampton, not far from his home, he suddenly had a vision that with all the violence certain to occur, he might well be killed. He stopped and called Cristina, confiding his fears to her. She urged him not to go if that was how he felt. It was, and he returned to East Hampton—the man who successfully maneuvered around a Chinese airport mined by the Japanese in 1944 having unaccountably lost his resolve to drive to Chicago in 1968. He regretted being away from the action, but at least he avoided being shot.

A small player in a world of essentially small profits, Grove remained a financially precarious enterprise from the start. Income rarely met expenses during the first ten years. Barney survived them by sinking his trust funds and the portion of his father's one-and-three-quarter-million-dollar estate that he inherited (most went to Mary) into the business. After that, some prescient buying of technology stocks as well as shrewd investment in East Hampton real estate—at one point, Barney owned more than a mile of ocean-front footage—produced the personal resources to help keep the company afloat. The prestigious writers Barney signed as Grove authors—in 1961, for example, he published Beckett, Pablo Neruda, Octavio Paz, and Harold Pinter, all of whom went on to win Nobel prizes—were far from bestsellers. If he took pride in Grove's "serious" list, he also took pleasure in his Victorian library of both vintage and contemporary pornography, which helped pay the bills. Sex and politics, as he liked to point out, were what Grove was about.

Those two elements came together in a single work—not a book but a movie—that would both constitute Grove's greatest financial success and ultimately—and ironically—lead to its financial collapse. The decisive turn of events began innocuously enough. At the 1967 Frankfurt Book Fair, Barney read an article in the *Manchester Guardian* about a film that had recently opened in Sweden to enormous controversy—and enormous popularity. Written and directed by Vilgot Sjöman, *I Am Curious (Yellow)* examines Swedish attitudes toward class, gender, and assorted social issues by having Lena, the female protagonist, go around Stockholm interviewing different characters to elicit their views and occasionally making love with her boyfriend. Sjöman, who appears in the movie, also includes footage of his talking to Martin Luther King, who happened to be visiting Stockholm during the filming, as well as a conversation with then minister of transportation (and later prime minister), Olaf Palme. Lena's examination of the real nature of Swedish society, by no means as classless as it liked to pretend, was provocative enough, but it was the sex, not the politics, that drove the Swedes to the theater. The film displays frontal nudity, and much feigned intercourse, some of it—even more shocking—in front of the Swedish king's palace. Approximately 1.3 million Swedes out of a population of 8 million swarmed to see it.

As with the *Tropic of Cancer*, whose sexual content he claimed not to notice, Barney always maintained that the film's political concerns primarily absorbed him rather than the hitherto forbidden glimpses on a major motion-picture screen of male and female genitalia. His avowal might be more credible if he hadn't, after learning about the film, sent Phyllis and Eberhard Kronhausen, eminent sexologists of the sixties and pals of his, to Sweden for their professional assessment as to whether they thought it appropriate for Grove's American distribution. Known familiarly around the Grove office for their erotic interests as Syphilis and Everhard, the Kronhausens had established their film criticism credentials with Barney several years earlier when Grove published their *The Sexually Responsive Woman*. The couple's expertise didn't come cheap: they somehow inveigled Barney into a contract that if they endorsed the film and he acquired it, they would receive 10 percent of the asking price. When word came back that the movie was "pretty good," Barney and Cristina immediately went off to Sweden and bought it on the spot for $100,000. The Kronhausens never made an easier $10,000.

Needless to say, Customs seized the film in New York, initiating the rhythm of harassment, confiscation, arrest, and court appearances across the country that Grove had become used to during the liberation of *Tropic of Cancer*. As theater operators were scrambling to keep their theaters open to the vast audiences lining up to see the film, Barney once again put Ed de Grazia in charge of Grove's litigation strategy after his success with *Naked Lunch.* He devised a scheme to resist the interference of local law authorities. Instead of going to court after summonses were issued, de Grazia suggested that in every city where the film was to be shown, lawyers be hired to resolve all litigation issues in advance of the screening. It would be expensive—de Grazia recommended that the lawyers receive 10 percent of the theater's take—but it worked. Everywhere Grove employed a lawyer before anything happened, nothing happened: eager viewers bought tickets without incident. The high-priced and well-compensated attorneys earned their keep. When Grove failed to organize legal support beforehand, there were trials and Grove lost. Barney's team was hoping, as had happened in the Henry Miller campaign, to get an appeal before the Supreme Court to put a definitive end to the obscenity hassle but had no luck. Finally, in 1969, a year and a half after the film arrived in the United States, a Grove defeat in Maryland prompted the Court to hear Grove's argument.

Barney was optimistic, particularly because he knew that Justice William O. Douglas, the Court's most liberal member, would be strongly on his side. After all, the previous year *Evergreen Review* had published a chapter from his provocative meditation on political dissent, *Points of Rebellion,* in which he defends the legitimacy of rebellion when a nation is oppressed by a government viewed by the people as no longer representing them. Strong stuff, especially during the Vietnam War. (In the midst of the 1970 impeachment proceedings against Doug-las, Congressman Gerald Ford waved the issue containing Douglas's article before the assembled members of the House of Representatives, declaring that the Justice was the kind of disreputable character who would choose to publish his work in such a flagrantly pornographic magazine.) Unfortunately, although Douglas's sympathies were certainly with Grove, his appearance in *Evergreen* required that he recuse himself from the deliberations, leaving the Court divided, 4-4. A split Supreme Court means the original, contested decision stands; to this day, though the film is available in cassettes and DVDs, it remains technically against the law to show *I Am Curious (Yellow)* in a movie theater.

By the time the judgment came down, it hardly mattered, as the film had already been enormously profitable through-out the country. Theater owners in major cities proved only too eager to book what had become known as "I Am Curi-ous (Money)." Swelling box-office receipts testified not to the insatiable American fascination with the Swedish social sys-tem but to the public's hunger to see things never before avail-able in legitimate movie houses. Although the movie would likely receive a PG rating today, in 1969 it was pure X-rated, a scandalous violation of conventional norms, permitting respectable citizens to witness a young Swedish woman kissing a flaccid penis. As Barney later said, he made a fortune "wag-ing cultural war" on behalf of *I Am Curious (Yellow)*. Upscale audiences, not simply the stereotypical ragged old men in rain-coats, made clear the broad nature of the film's allure. Barney cited the positive publicity generated by newspaper coverage of an argument between Aristotle and Jackie Onassis who had gone to see the movie at 57th Street in New York. Jackie hated it and wanted to leave; Aristotle wanted to stay. When Jackie stormed out, Aristotle kept his bodyguards with him, leaving Jackie alone and vulnerable to the pursuit of a photographer who followed her out of the theater. She asserted her right to privacy by swatting him with an umbrella, causing him some distress but happily, at least from Barney's point of view, calling even more attention to the film.

Barney lamented his inexperience in negotiating the arcana of movie theater accounting. He felt that obscure bookkeeping practices he never fully grasped deprived Grove of substantial income that was rightfully his. Still, he estimated that *I Am Curious (Yellow)* took in approximately fourteen million dollars at the box office nationwide, adding between six and seven million to Grove's coffers. Suddenly, and for the first time, Grove was awash with money. Stymied by its inability to find a theater in Minneapolis to show the film, for example, Grove simply bought its own theater there. Barney had picked a gigantic winner for his small company. A fiscally sound future beckoned. The windfall, however, turned out, in Barney's words, to be "a disaster for us in many ways." The easy money he made from the film suggested a painless method to fund his publishing venture in the future: simply buy lots of foreign films and distribute them nationally, channeling the profits into signing up the authors and putting out the books that mattered to him. A perfectly sensible plan, with one horrendous miscalculation.

Despite Barney's insistence on the film's fascinating political dimensions, its immense success had to do with the public's perception that it offered alleged pornographic satisfactions, not illuminating social analysis. When independent theater owners appreciated that the masses were climbing over each other to see it, they stopped booking other interesting foreign movies and recast their art film theaters instead to show inexpensive, money-making porno flicks. After spending hundreds of thousands of dollars purchasing films across Europe, Barney was left with no buyers. "We killed our market," Barney later recognized. "There had been a big market for foreign films in this country, and suddenly it was gone. The art film houses all closed up overnight, in 1970."

The obliteration of a once profitable market was one unintended negative consequence of *I Am Curious (Yellow's)* success, but there were others. Grove's new affluence in the late sixties, based largely, but not entirely, on the film (there were, for example, substantial profits from *Games People Play* and *Malcolm X)*, raised the question of how best to invest the surplus cash that was piling up. Barney sought responsible advice, and the strategic wisdom he received from different sources all pointed in the same direction: real estate. A providential answer, or so it struck Barney at the time, as Grove had for years stuffed far too many people into far too little space, with crowded offices in two different buildings, the four top floors of 80 University Place and, in 1967, two floors of 52 East 11th Street, which Barney outfitted—at considerable expense—with a 154-seat theater and his own lushly decorated, full-scale public bar, to which he would repair at the end of the day to begin sipping his rum and cokes. The Black Circle Bar functioned as a dedicated money-loser from the start, both because he had no idea how to run the drinking business and because the bartenders and waiters were committed to ripping him off. But he loved it nevertheless, the idea as well as the reality, even if it taught him the painful truth that it is less expensive to drink at somebody else's establishment.

The need for expansion remained great, and if that corresponded with shrewd investment tactics, so much the better. A six-story, 32,000-square-foot building on Mercer and Bleecker Streets in Greenwich Village was available; in 1969 Grove bought it and began extensive renovations. Although Barney had to borrow heavily to afford it, his decision seemed to have no downside. Grove needed the space; Barney could get the money; and perhaps most reassuring, NYU, with its voracious appetite for acquiring additional buildings, was across the street, so if anything went wrong, Grove would have instant access to a wealthy, interested buyer. The man with the whim of steel appeared to have acted prudently to support the company's healthy expansion.

Work on the building began in the fall of 1969. When it came to matters of design, Barney's capitalistic side trumped his communistic concern for the downtrodden. He liked things to be nice and, after the years of struggle, was prepared to pay for the amenities appropriate to an enterprise that from its fledgling inventory of three books had grown into a prestigious New York publishing firm. His architects, Heery and Heery, won the 1970 Interior Design award sponsored by Architectural Record for their work. Spacious offices, filled with sleek new furniture, replaced the dowdy look of the old cramped cubicles, central air-conditioning guaranteed editorial comfort, and an impressive G-shaped arched entranceway through which people came into the building declared the formidable presence of Grove Press. Perhaps most self-indulgently, Barney installed two elevators, one exclusively for him (though senior editors like Seaver and Jordan could occasionally hitch a ride) and one for all the rest. The need for an executive elevator was explained by some to speak to Barney's essential shyness and his desire not to be trapped in a confined space with people he didn't know.

The building was completed in 1970. With its newfound solvency and architectural chic, Grove stood poised for a prosperous third decade. "The Smart Little Company That Can Do No Wrong," as one Wall Street broker celebrated it when it went public in 1967, was well housed and on it way.

The ancient Greeks had a word for it—*peripeteia*—which means roughly, "a sudden turn of events or an unexpected reversal." It applies to Oedipus's trajectory in Sophocles' *Oedipus Rex* from adored king and savior of Thebes to an outcast guilty of patricide and incest; it describes the descent into chaos that Barney experienced after purchasing the building. The New York real-estate market, it turned out, was not a foolproof investment after all. A precipitous collapse at the end of the sixties meant that Mercer Street was declining in value even as Grove poured millions of dollars into its renovation.

It also meant that no one wanted to take it off Grove's hands, at any price. The publishing business in general and Grove in particular did not fare any better than real estate. No longer propped up by the unsustainable profits of *I Am Curious (Yellow)*, Grove's income suffered grievously. Mounting cost overruns on the building and the need to meet mortgage payments strained already depleted resources. In 1970, it lost more than $2.3 million. By December 1971, its liabilities exceeded its assets by close to five million dollars. When its stock price, which had actually reached $40, tumbled to under a dollar, Standard and Poor refused any longer to list it. By 1973, it was selling at six cents a share.

8

A MURDER STORY; SOME STOLEN FINGERPRINTS

The toxic combination of dwindling income and uncontrollable expenses didn't need any assistance in bringing Grove down, but Barney was soon besieged from other directions as well.

The 1968 grenade attack became a kind of metaphoric prelude to the traumas that followed. Barney thought of 1970 as the year an "attempt was made to murder Grove Press." The assault came from a coalition of unlikely forces: the Joint Board of the Fur, Leather, and Machine Workers (FLM), a division of the Amalgamated Meat Cutters and Butcher Workers of North America (a member union of the AFL-CIO); and a group of feminists, enraged at Barney's alleged sexist behavior and publishing practices.

Barney became indignant when he learned in early April that the Fur, Leather, and Machine Workers' Organizing

Committee had started an effort to unionize Grove's editorial
staff. That a publishing house with Grove's legitimate radical credentials—opposing the Vietnam War, supporting the
Cuban revolution, standing up for Black Power, empathizing
with the oppressed peoples of the world—should be singled out
for a unionizing campaign struck him as both bizarre and suspicious. Barney had a theory he could never prove, but which
he never gave up: the CIA or the FBI encouraged the union
to try to organize Grove in order to disrupt its functioning and
cast it as "anti-union, anti-left, sexist, and a Capitalist profi-
teer." Whether his suspicions were true or not, it is certainly
the case that ever since Barney at age twelve allegedly praised
Mussolini, one agency or another of the government—Army
Intelligence, the FBI and the CIA—were treating Barney as a
subversive type to be carefully watched. And with the emer-
gence of Grove and *Evergreen* as countercultural sources of
energy, publishing writers who took issue with established
authority on every conceivable subject—political, social,
moral, sexual—it would not be irrational to think that the
government would breathe more easily if Grove ceased to
exist. Such was the plausible argument Barney created for
himself. Barney later stated that Henry Foner, president of the
FLM, admitted to him that he never entirely understood why
Grove, of all publishing houses, should have been chosen for a
unionization drive, and agreed that it might well have been an
FBI-instigated project.

On April 8, 1970, the union called an organizing meeting.
About to fly to Europe on a film-buying expedition, Barney

insisted that those employees who showed up at the meeting be fired immediately. Dick Seaver and others made efforts to dissuade him, on the grounds that firing workers because of pro-union sympathies could be held against Grove in any future litigation, but Barney was adamant. More than angry, he felt betrayed that people could so misconstrue the unique personal culture of Grove to think that they needed the bureaucratic structure of a union to improve their working lives. After all, it was not a regular corporation like the others, interested only in profit, but something resembling an extended family sharing the same liberal values, intent on changing the world for the better. Or even perhaps as a team, with Barney as the impassioned quarterback calling the signals in the heat of the game, rather than as the distant CEO plotting long-term strategy. He expected his players to understand his mission and his method.

On April 9 and 10, for what he argued were purely economic reasons, Barney fired nine employees who had attended the union meeting. Then he and Fred Jordan boarded a plane to Denmark. On Monday, April 13, he called his secretary, Judith Schmidt, to see how things were going. She replied everything was fine, except that she was speaking to him from the fifth floor, instead of his sixth-floor office. When he inquired why, she informed him that his office had been taken over by some two dozen women, brandishing buttons that read, WE ARE FURIOUS (YELLOW), who were protesting the firings as well as Grove's exploitation of women as evident in the pornography it published. Apoplectic—and terrified that they might destroy Grove's precious archive of irreplaceable letters with its authors—Barney directed his staff to get them out. Not surprisingly, none of his editors expressed interest in such a confrontation, and Barney finally had to order the police to be called in. The occupiers initially declared they would only leave if escorted out by policewomen. When not enough female officers could be found to accomplish this, the protestors agreed to vacate the premises under the authority of policemen. Fifteen left voluntarily; nine insisted on being arrested and booked.

Meanwhile, broadsheets were distributed charging Grove with the following crimes against women:

> Grove Press and its subsidiaries, *Evergreen Review*, Grove Films and other corporate enterprises have earned millions off the basic theme of humiliating, degrading and dehumanizing women through sado-masochistic literature, pornographic films and oppressive and exploitative practices against its own female employees. (For example, women employees are fired for their political beliefs and are denied medical benefits for their children.)

To redress these grievances, the demands included that "all publications of books and magazines, and all distribution of films that degrade women must be stopped immediately"; that Barney Rosset must open all financial records to public scrutiny and that Grove's profits be redirected to the following: twenty-four-hour-a-day free child-care centers; a fund for recently divorced and widowed women to help them recover; a fund to establish free abortion and birth-control clinics; a bail fund to free each month a minimum of one hundred political prisoners (mostly prostitutes) from the Women's House of Detention; a fund to meet the needs, medical, and otherwise, of rape and abuse victims. In addition, profits from the *Autobiography of Malcolm X* must go to the black community, to be distributed by the black women of that community; and profits on books written by Latin and South American revolutionaries such as Castro, Che, and Debray must go to the people of the Spanish-speaking community, to be distributed by the women in that community.

Finally, and arguably most painful of all to Barney, "A company-wide Cooperative must be established to end 'one-dirty-old-man rule' at Grove Press. Women must control 51 percent of all decisions, editorial, and otherwise."

Overnight, the little company that could do no wrong, that had gamely resisted oppression in every form and at whatever cost, had been transformed into the very thing it abhorred: a callous opponent of workers' rights, an exploiter of women, a racist, brutal employer prepared to call upon the power of the state to crush legitimate protest. The hero of the left now found himself pilloried by the left—a savage irony Barney had difficulty digesting. A vitriolic manifesto underscored the women's specific economic demands:

No more business as usual for Grove Press and *Evergreen Magazine*!

No more using of women's bodies as filth-objects (both black and white) to sell a phony radicalism-for-profit to the middle-American-white-male!

No more using of women's bodies to rip off enormous profits for a few wealthy capitalist dirty old straight white men, such as Barney Rosset!

No more using of women as shit workers to produce material that degrades them; no more underpaid, demeaning, degrading work for anyone!

No more scapegoating of women for daring to demand the rights and respect that are—for any human being—inalienable!

No more wearing of a radical mask by these exploiters to cover the sexist leer, the racist smirk, the boss-man's frown!

No more union busting by rich-man Rosset!

Fact: one woman worker was denied the health insurance coverage for her child that is automatically given to male workers who have children. The sole reason: she was a woman!

No more mansions on Long Island for boss-man Rosset and his executive yes-men flunkies, segregated mansions built with extortionist profits from selling *The Autobiography of Malcolm X*, a bestseller—and not one black welfare mother a penny better off after millions of copies made Rosset rich!

No more Latin American executive junkets for the rich men who sell the books of Che, Bosch, Debray to get rich while the Latin cities they visit are choked with hungry babies!

No more peddling of Grove movies that offer nudity as "sexual liberation" but present women as "hung-up" and men as "liberated," and that force women to act out their bestialized oppression while the whole world is watching, making Rosset rich!

No more financing of male-left radicals in cushy lifestyles by selling their hypocritical radicalism to *Evergreen* for lots of money—a magazine that with *Playboy* is one of the heaviest anti-women propaganda machines in the country!

No more male radicals who can ignore the oppression of women—as sex objects, as workers, as union organizers, as feminists, as radicals, as revolutionaries, as socialists—and continue to reap profits based on the degradation of women!!!

No more, no more, no more. Shut it down. Close it up. We want reparations!

Grove rapidly plunged into terminal disrepair, driven by its diminishing income, constant picketing, bomb threats, fire alarms, massive internal dissension, and corrosive publicity. Buyers of Grove books and readers of *Evergreen* were urged to stop supporting them in their corruption. Colleagues from other publishing houses who had never liked Barney in the first place gladly joined in the anti-Grove demonstrations. "Grove Press has sued for freedom of speech throughout the country," André Schiffrin of Pantheon wrote on a flyer, "What a sad irony that they should have kept it out of their own offices." John Simon of Random House accused Grove of "felony arrests and union busting." (Barney called Bob Bernstein, president of Random House, whom he didn't know, and told him that if he didn't prevent Simon from participating in the chanting and picketing, he personally was going to organize a group to take over

Random House, by force. Simon stopped.) Liberal writers who had been published by Barney made clear that they no longer relished any association with him. Columnist Jack Newfield, in offering his public resignation from *Evergreen*, accused the magazine of being "clearly guilty of exploiting and dehumanizing women." Resigning as an *Evergreen* contributing editor, African American intellectual Julius Lester immediately wrote to Barney, "I have not had the opportunity to hear your side of the story and that really doesn't matter. The summary firings and arrests speak very clearly for themselves. It is quite obvious that for Grove, revolution is a matter of profit, not of life-style, behavior or attitude toward others."

As the turmoil continued, Barney cooperated with the leadership of the FLM to expedite union elections. Work essentially stopped as the union held numerous meetings to advertise the benefits of membership. When people weren't meeting, they were arguing with each other. No one was thinking about books. The union stressed job security, provision for day care, a minimum wage. Management retaliated by calling attention to the reactionary nature of the union, the fact that its constitution prohibited members from believing in violence or overthrowing the government. The so-called left-wing union proved to be well to the right of the liberal Grove Press. Never mind that butchers, furriers, and the like would seem to have little in common with book publishers, Grove argued, do you really want to join a union where you can't be a Black Panther? The answer, delivered on April 30, was a resounding no, 86-34. Grove would not become the first house to be unionized. After the vote, Barney consented to rehire—if only temporarily—the nine workers who had been fired for their presence at the initial union meeting.

Early in May, Barney and his lawyer, Cy Rembar, attended the court hearing for the occupiers who had opted to be arrested. Of the nine, only two were employed at Grove: Robin Morgan and Emily Goodman. Morgan, the group's leader, was an ardent feminist and political activist who had been an editor at Grove for about two years; Goodman, who served as the women's lawyer, had worked as staff counsel for Grove and had been hired, as Barney ruefully noted, "because I wanted to be in the forefront of using women legal professionals."

Complete with two crying babies, one of them Robin Morgan's, the courtroom scene had all the trappings of comic opera. Emily Goodman went before the judge and accused the police of having stolen their fingerprints, which she demanded be returned. She also insisted that the court immediately establish a child-care center in the courtroom. Meanwhile, Barney and Rembar, understanding the public relations disaster that would ensue for Grove if the women were found guilty and sentenced to prison terms (Barney could just imagine the derisive headlines that would follow Grove's hounding its own female workers to jail), desperately tried to get the judge to drop the case. The women, on the other hand, earnestly sought a guilty verdict, to dramatize the point about Grove's dreadful treatment of them. They were joined by the DA, who wanted the case brought to judgment. He argued that the police would no longer feel comfortable making arrests if they thought nothing

would result from them. So it was Grove, represented by lawyer Rembar, arguing to free the women, while the women,
represented by lawyer Goodman and abetted by the DA, were
pushing for conviction. During the proceedings, Barney spoke
to one of the arresting officers, who assured him that dropping
the charges would not affect his ability to perform his police
responsibilities in the future. Based on this information, Rembar called the officer to the stand, where he repeated his position, negating the DA's warnings that letting the women go
would discourage the police from fulfilling their duties. Much
screaming, from infants and principals, filled the courtroom,
until the judge, clearly unable to endure the oddity of it all,
looked around the room, announced his agreement with Rembar, and dismissed the case. Rembar later said that defending
the women who didn't want to be defended constituted one of
his finest hours as an attorney.

9

DECLINE AND FALL

The year of the attempted murder of Grove did not result in Grove's death, but it inflicted serious wounds from which the business could never recover. Although Barney took some comfort in his murder scenario, depicting a courageous publishing house set upon by rabid feminists, dogged union organizers, and cunning government plotters, in truth the injuries were also self-inflicted. Irresponsible fiscal management—high mortgages, extravagant renovations, and debilitating cost overruns on the Mercer Street building, the sublimely self-indulgent and expensive bar, the enormous investment in films that were never distributed—was destructive enough. The disruptive consequences of the demonstrations and takeover, combined with a general economic downturn and a collapsing real-estate market, guaranteed that Grove would require emergency medical support that Barney could no longer provide. The personal funds he had poured into the company from his successful investment in technology stocks and the sale of valuable Southampton waterfront property had dried up. Books were not generating enough profit, and Barney had exhausted his alternative funding sources.

Faced with the intractable problem of diminishing income and swelling costs, Barney had no choice but to slash the scale of the operation. He reduced the number of Grove employees from one hundred and forty or so to about a dozen, firing three stalwarts who had been crucial to its growth: Nat Sobel, sales manager; Morrie Goldfischer, director of publicity; and Jules Geller, director of the education division. (Dick Seaver and Fred Jordan, his two indispensable editorial colleagues, left on their own, Dick in 1971, Fred in 1977.) He evacuated the elegant quarters of the Mercer Street building that he had only recently moved into, retreating first to the uncomfortably crowded conditions of East 11th Street, still under lease to Grove, and later, to the even smaller space of his own home at 196 West Houston Street. When he finally found a buyer for Mercer Street, he received only a fraction of what he had spent and still owed on it. Unable any longer to afford the costs of book distribution, he worked out a deal with his friend Jason Epstein who arranged to have Random House take on this activity for Grove. Epstein's intervention was more than a friendly favor: Barney had to renounce not just a portion of the profits, but even more painfully, the rights to some of Grove's precious backlist titles, like *The Autobiography of Malcolm X* and *Games People Play*. A hard bargain, but one he felt he had to make. And in 1971, he ceased publishing *Evergreen Review*. Together, these measures plunged Barney into a permanent survival mode, scrambling primarily to stay alive rather than actually flourish. Assessing his career after he was forced to sell Grove in 1985, Barney offered a harsh appraisal of his failure to keep the business going: "I think we published a lot of good books. A lot. But I ultimately goofed terribly." (Al Goldstein, *Screw* magazine's publisher and arguably this country's leading guru of pornography in the late sixties and early seventies, celebrated him as "the worst, most fucked-up businessman in America.")

Goofing, as he undoubtedly did, particularly in his relative indifference to serious financial oversight, there is also an ironic sense in which he was undone by his own successes. By the time things began to fall apart, the upstart, provocative company had metastasized into a multimedia operation with a film division, a theater, a book club, a magazine, and an education division catering to colleges and universities. His tiny enterprise with its radical instincts had become an establishment institution with large ambitions. The cultural edginess that originally defined it got blurred in its expansion, and other publishers began to move in on both Grove authors and the Grove audience. Daring sexual content, once the Grove exception, could now be found everywhere. Having emancipated the reading public from oppressive puritanical constraints, Grove necessarily lost some of the uniqueness that had characterized it earlier. And with the damage done to its progressive image by the unionizing fiasco and the feminist takeover, Barney's best efforts could not quite manage to put Grove back together again.

The company muddled through the seventies, but only just. Creative tax shelters devised by lawyer Richard Gallen played a major role in keeping Grove afloat. What income book sales generated went to creditors, instead of providing competitive advances to acquire new and challenging writers. Dependent on, but also crippled by, the distribution arrangement with Random House, lacking the support of an *Evergreen* magazine to help call attention to itself, and with a vastly depleted staff, Grove lost visibility. Joining the underground no longer seemed so sexy, so much a part of one's cutting-edge, countercultural bona fides. Grove volumes on the bookshelves counted for less than they formerly did.

As Barney struggled to make the finances work, he continued to be consumed by the role he insisted the government played in bringing Grove down. On January 9, 1975, in an effort to engage the *New York Times*'s investigative reporter Seymour Hersh in exploring the connection between the CIA and Grove's difficulties, Barney wrote, over Fred Jordan's signature, a four-page letter detailing the many reasons why the Agency would welcome the closing down of a subversive publishing house. Ostensibly supplying evidence for Hersh to consider, the document actually provides a concise summary of some of Barney's proudest radical achievements and provocations over the previous decade.

In a section entitled "Cause for CIA operations against Grove Press," Jordan (Barney) lists the following:

a. Grove Press and the magazine it published, *Evergreen Review*, were among the first in the United States to take a determined stand against the war in Vietnam.

b. Grove Press published many of the original texts of such Third World authors as Frantz Fanon, and Régis Debray which became handbooks for the anti-colonialist movement in Asia, South America, and Africa, and had an incalculable effect on the black movement as well as the radical movement inside the United States.

c. Grove Press was the publisher of many of the original rebellious voices of the Black movement in the United States, including Malcolm X, Imamu Baraka (LeRoi Jones), and others.

d. Grove Press and *Evergreen Review* were among the first to publish reports of the CIA involvement in the military operations in Bolivia against Che Guevara, and Grove Press was among the first to publish the writings of Che Guevara in the United States. Grove Press was also intimately involved in the efforts to publish Che Guevara's diary; Joe Liss, an employee of Grove, went to Bolivia in 1968, followed by both Barney Rosset and myself several weeks later. We succeeded in getting important portions of the diary before anyone else did, including information about CIA involvement in the killing of Guevara.

e. Grove Press published, among others, an exposé of the US involvement in the overthrow of Juan Bosch in the Dominican Republic, by Juan Bosch himself, which was a serious attack on the power of the Pentagon and its interference in the affairs of Latin American countries.

f. *Evergreen Review* was one of the most outspoken critics of the government's prosecution of the Chicago Seven and one of its reports on the tampering by the government with the Chicago Seven became a cornerstone in the appeal of the sentence which was finally overturned.

g. Grove Press and *Evergreen Review* were among the first to publish the writings of Fidel Castro in the United States, and to report on the accomplishments of the revolution in Cuba. In February, 1970, Barney Rosset and Richard Seaver, then Managing Editor of Grove Press, visited Cuba at the invitation of the Cuban Government in order to negotiate for the release in the United States of several Cuban films. Upon their return to the US they regained admittance into the country only after difficulties at Kennedy Airport.

h. Grove Press was the publisher of Soviet spy Kim Philby's memoirs, *My Silent War*, which, as you have reported, first exposed the role of Jim Angleton in the CIA.

Including the rocket-propelled grenade attack, the unionizing efforts of the FLM, and the feminist sit-in of his office as activities that smacked of CIA involvement, Barney concludes, "the conjunction of events, the evidence in hand, and an objective evaluation of the results of these events justifies further investigation as to whether or not there was a CIA drive to silence, in violation of its charter as well as the First Amendment guarantees of a free press, a major US publisher of information and views in opposition to the then promulgated policy of the US government."

Hersh, who the previous year had written a long piece in the *Times* exposing the CIA's illegal domestic spying, chose not to pursue the Grove case. Barney, however, would not relinquish his conviction that the CIA played a significant part in the company's troubles. His suspicions about the CIA's interest in Grove's demise were unexpectedly confirmed in June of 1975 from an unlikely source: the Commission on CIA Activities within the United States, known as the Rockefeller Commission, which documented the extent to which the CIA monitored and gathered information about Grove Press. The Agency had opened a file on Grove when it issued in 1968 the memoirs of Kim Philby, the British intelligence agent who was actually working for the Russians. As the commission's report revealed, the publication of the Philby book alerted the

Chaos analysts (the group within the CIA investigating foreign contacts with American dissidents) to the threat posed by Grove. By virtue of the memoir and *Evergreen's* political materials "rapidly circulating into many foreign countries," Grove had become, in the eyes of the Agency, an "internal security" matter. Thereafter, Chaos never ceased its scrutiny of the company.

Barney immediately sought the release of all the CIA papers relating to Grove. In July, when not all were forthcoming, Barney announced a $10 million civil suit against the CIA. He charged them with withholding material to conceal their criminal activities in attempting to interfere with the constitutional rights of Grove and Barney to express their political views. To the ten million in compensatory damages for lost revenue, he added $100,000 in punitive damages from each of the defendants. The list of alleged culprits was neither small nor undistinguished: "George Bush, William E. Colby, James Schlesinger, Richard Helms, John A. McCone, William F. Raborn Jr., James J. Angleton, Raymond Rocca, William J. Hood, Newton S. Miler, Thomas Karamessines, Richard Ober, John Doe, Richard Doe, Jane Doe and other Unknown Employees of the Central Intelligence Agency and other Agencies of the Federal Government."

The suit failed to produce any money, but it did force the release of previously restricted files that explicitly indicated the government's concern with Grove. The files did not, however, provide the evidence that Barney hoped would show the CIA's active participation in the bombing and attempted unionizing of the company. However, he continued to believe the CIA did more than simply observe and gather information. In 2000, he hired Richard Cummings, a lawyer and writer, to examine the files that had been obtained from various government agencies to see if illegal meddling in Grove's affairs could be demonstrated. Cummings, try as he might, could not definitely establish proof of guilt. But his overall assessment of how much grief Barney had caused the government must still have given him considerable pleasure:

> At the outset, it is significant to note that the abundance of material provided by the US government agencies, including the US Army, the FBI, and the CIA, however censored, leads to the ineluctable conclusion that you have been one of the most scrutinized US citizens in the annals of American intelligence gathering, but that you gave as good as you got. They had a very hard time with you and never did figure you out. Accused of "disaffection" while in military service, you proved yourself to be a consummate patriot. Suspected of procommunist sympathies, you emerged as one of the country's leading libertarian entrepreneurs who revolutionized the publishing industry by turning a tiny, defunct press into a highly profitable and dynamic operation that introduced many great authors and poets to American readers.

Cummings added that Grove Press and *Evergreen Review* had engaged "your imagination; they challenged the status quo and brought the FBI and the CIA to see you as an institutional threat. But before that, you caught the attention of the FBI and Military intelligence simply by being yourself."

Barney being himself, as Cummings observed, was more than enough to occupy the attention not just of innumerable government investigators but of large chunks of the American reading public as well.

10

"WHO IS THE CEO OF GROVE?"

Barney required roughly a dozen years to settle his debts. By the time he did, in the early 1980s, it had become clear to him that he needed a substantial infusion of cash if he was to restore Grove to healthy financial shape. Book sales alone would not be enough: the frontlist was not as distinguished as it had been; and the profits from the marvelous backlist were being drained off by the distribution arrangement with Random House. What to do? When his efforts to find investors prepared to put money into the company failed, he realized he would have to consider a more radical step: the actual sale of Grove.

In the fall of 1984, Barney's hunt for a buyer meshed with a British publisher's hunt for an American outpost for his business. For several years, George Weidenfeld, a well-connected émigré turned British aristocrat (Baron Weidenfeld

of Chelsea), had been looking to expand to these shores his
Weidenfeld and Nicolson publishing house—the company he
ran with Nigel Nicolson, son of English writers Harold Nicolson and Vita Sackville-West. A man who chose his friends
and partners with exquisite care, Weidenfeld, whom Barney
described as "an astonishing, cigar-chomping hippopotamus
with small feet, bulging eyes, exquisitely tailored suits and a
puzzling Austrian accent," had become close to Ann Getty,
wife of Gordon Getty, heir to oil tycoon J. Paul Getty's bil-
lions. Ann had long harbored dreams of involving herself in
American publishing, fantasies that Weidenfeld strategically
nourished. By the time he contacted Barney in 1984, Weidenfeld had worked out an understanding with Ann: she would
provide the money to enable Weidenfeld to purchase Grove
and move to New York. She would then become president of
the new entity, to be called the Wheatland Corporation, after
the name of her hometown in California; Weidenfeld would
be the chairman. Although at the start she would have no real
executive responsibilities, after ten years or so he would retire
and Ann would take over the management of the company.
With Ann's resources committed to making the plan a reality,
all that was necessary was Barney's agreement.

Barney was surprised to receive an invitation from Weidenfeld in September to meet him for a drink at the Hotel Carlyle
where he was staying. While he had known Weidenfeld profes-
sionally ever since he entered the publishing business, they had
rarely socialized. He was even more surprised when Weidenfeld
explained that he and Ann wanted to purchase Grove, while

keeping Barney on to run the company as he always had. Barney had entertained offers from publishers in the past, Putnam and Prentice-Hall, to name two, but none were as generous as this one: $2 million. And none had come at a more precarious point for the company. According to Barney, "There was no cash flow, we were just spinning our wheels."

The economic incentives to make the deal were great, but so were the anxieties. Ever since he had bought out Phelps and Balcomb in 1951, Barney had worked only for Barney. The thought of ceding authority to someone else after thirty-three years of doing things solely his way was, to say the least, unsettling. Having run his own superbly non-bureaucratic organization, could he fit into a more conventional corporate structure? Would Grove's distinctive culture survive being folded into a larger enterprise?

Barney agonized throughout the fall and winter, but the financial imperatives and Weidenfeld's assurances that Barney would remain the guiding spirit of Grove finally prevailed. In March 1985, Barney returned to the Carlyle to work out the specific terms. But before he actually signed the contract, Barney experienced a change of mind. He had decided not to sell. He couldn't quiet the doubts he harbored about Weidenfeld's trustworthiness. When Weidenfeld's people asked what could encourage him to close the deal, Barney replied, the profits from Grove's "Victorian Library," the adult and romance portion of the company that produced its erotic books. As the income from the Library generated approximately $250,000 in 1984, Barney was not negotiating about an insignificant amount of money. Weidenfeld had no intention of letting Barney cream off such a valuable piece of the business. He offered Barney 20 percent of the VL's profits. After considerable haggling, Weidenfeld capitulated to Barney's demands to increase his share to a third. Barney's objections then evaporated, and the Wheatland Corporation, headed by Weidenfeld and Getty, became the new owner of Grove Press.

Barney was under the impression that Weidenfeld had promised to keep him on as Grove's CEO for at least five years but matters were not that clear-cut. No such clause existed in the contract. Whatever Barney's understanding of his tenure, the actual language of the agreement specified that "Rosset shall serve as chief executive officer of the Corporation [Grove] until such time as the Corporation's Board of Directors shall designate a successor chief executive officer. Thereafter Rosset shall serve the Corporation as a Senior Editor." The contract goes on to spell out Barney's responsibilities as CEO. They include activities Barney had probably never performed while Grove belonged to him and certainly had the least aptitude or taste for: "proper conduct of day-to-day business . . . preparation of budgets and financial reports," and "their proper implementation." And all under the control of the board of directors, though Barney insisted that Weidenfeld had stressed that the directors would not involve themselves very aggressively in the company's affairs. Barney remained convinced that even with a board to monitor his behavior and the selection of a Wheatland CEO to exercise authority over his decisions at Grove, he would effectively be running the business as in the past.

Such was Barney's understanding, but not Weidenfeld's or that of Dan Green, a publishing veteran whom Weidenfeld hired in October to serve as Wheatland CEO. Green had worked for twenty-three years at Simon & Shuster, where he had served as publicity director, publisher, and president of their trade division. While Barney had ruled Grove from the start by instinct and impulse, Green had grown up in a sober environment of sales projections, budgets, and editorial meetings. The two men saw the world of publishing entirely differently. Green had no affection for the creative chaos that defined Grove; Barney viewed with contempt the tight organization and administrative decorum that marked a "respectable" publishing house.

Obviously not a match made in heaven. At his initial meeting with Barney after the sale, Green instantly realized there would be terrible problems. Although Green understood that Weidenfeld wanted him to exercise financial control over Grove, Barney spoke as if they were simply two independent managers who would direct their companies precisely as they saw fit. They would talk to one another, but Green appreciated that Barney intended to make his own decisions, irrespective of Green's input.

It is hard to imagine why Weidenfeld thought such a peculiar arrangement might work. The two CEOs fought from the start about everything: which books from the backlist should be reprinted; how they should be advertised; the relationship between the sales and editorial divisions at Grove. After seven months of bickering, it became clear to Green there was no way he could control Barney. If such was Weidenfeld's hope, it could not possibly happen. Green's grim analysis convinced Weidenfeld that he had made a serious mistake. It was time to invoke the escape clause he had built into Barney's contract: he could remain CEO of Grove until the board should choose a successor, after which he would function as senior editor. On April 3, 1986, Weidenfeld's lawyer asked Barney to attend a Wheatland board meeting at the corporation's Park Avenue law offices. Barney had bad vibes about what was to take place when he arrived, which were made worse when he realized as the meeting began that the directors— Getty, Weidenfeld, Marc Leland, and Arnold Schaab—seemed to be referring to Dan Green as Grove's CEO, not him. Puzzled, Barney wrote on a piece of paper, "Who is the CEO of Grove?," a question he stared at for about thirty seconds before he put it directly to Weidenfeld. "Dan," the stunning reply came back. Barney expressed his amazement to Leland that they could do this to him. Leland responded dismissively that Barney surely knew this was going to happen from the moment he signed the contract. Barney later accused Green of chiming in that he had always found Barney unpleasantly "iconoclastic" and "an onerous burden."

Perhaps he should have expected it, but he didn't. Fred Jordan later said he couldn't believe that Barney would assume he could sell his company and remain in charge of it. "Once you get rid of it, you are out," he declared. He thought Barney was nuts to imagine he might continue. Barney, however, was genuinely in shock. He lashed out at Green, calling him "a hatchet man" and warning him that he would be "the next to go." He looked at Weidenfeld, whose head, according to

Barney, "was going bob bob bob, up and down like crazy, like he was agreeing with me." Barney's account of the meeting then added a touch of surrealism to the trauma of his demotion. Having just absorbed the bad news, Barney reported that the door to the office suddenly opened and in walked the great Italian tenor Luciano Pavarotti, to embrace both Getty and Weidenfeld. "I couldn't leave New York without seeing Ann," he blurted out. Barney, transfixed, glared at him silently, until he came over to introduce himself to the now former CEO. Obviously sensing the awkwardness of the moment, Pavarotti commented that perhaps this was not such a good time to have interrupted the meeting and departed. Weidenfeld states—and Green agrees— that it was not Pavarotti but the equally distinguished Spanish tenor Placido Domingo who hugged them and promptly left. Whichever tenor walked out might be said to have appropriately brought down the curtain on Barney's career at Grove. Barney left the office several minutes later.

In retrospect, Barney felt he never should have succumbed to Weidenfeld's financial blandishments. While he was fond of Ann, he should have honored his skepticism about Weidenfeld's motives in dropping down from the heavens to save the business: "So when this guy Weidenfeld came along and said, 'Oh I've got this woman who's got all the money in the world and she's gonna give it all to me, and I want you. You can do whatever you want. I'll give you all this money to run the company.' I was sucked in. And then thrown out. Weidenfeld was a master con man. I shouldn't have been surprised. He has a great talent for taking you in and making you feel immune. He told me exactly what he was going to do to everyone and then he did it to me. And that in a nutshell was that."

If the structure of two dueling CEOs was a bad idea, Barney as a senior editor reporting to the man who replaced him was even worse. Few people were less constitutionally able to accept a subordinate role than Barney, and he certainly was not about to begin by deferring to Green. In June, he filed a $7 million breach-of-contract suit against Weidenfeld and Getty. Their lawyers didn't think Barney had much of a case, but they were reluctant to entangle the new publishers in complicated litigation. A placated Barney was a better alternative. Knowing Barney's enthusiasm for Grove's Victorian Library, Weidenfeld offered to carve it out of the company and sell it to him separately for $250,000 over a ten-year period. A good price, in return for which Barney dropped his suit. He then signed a letter, drafted by Weidenfeld, severing his connection with Grove and wishing the new owners well. He also agreed that for any book he might want to publish in a future business enterprise (except for those erotic volumes appropriate to the Victorian Library), he would extend to Grove the option to publish it first. A curious provision, designed, according to Leland, to guarantee peace between Barney and his old company, but clearly serving to constrict Barney's editorial free will. Barney thought it bizarre but consented because he assumed it would not be taken seriously.

With that, Barney closed the book on his thirty-five-year tenure at Grove as one of America's indomitable cultural revolutionaries. But not before trying to reclaim Grove from those who had gotten rid of him. Shortly after his dismissal, in the spring of 1986, he fashioned an offer of $4.5 million to buy the company back, more than twice the amount he had received for it. But Weidenfeld and Getty were not inclined to give up their newly established publishing base in New York and refused the bid. Money, in any case, meant very little to J. P. Getty's daughter-in-law.

A Grove Press without Barney seemed unnatural to many, not just to Barney. His admirers circulated a petition asking Wheatland either to permit Barney to run the company independently or to sell it to owners who might. Authors, editors, agents, and theatrical personalities signed, including Samuel Beckett, William Burroughs, Allen Ginsberg, Hubert Selby Jr., John Rechy, Herbert Gold, Harold Pinter, William Kunstler, Marguerite Duras, Lyle Stuart, Joseph Papp, and Eugene Ionesco, among others. Beckett, Barney's dear friend for more than thirty years, did more than add his name. When Barney told Sam in May of 1986, that he intended to stay in publishing, even without Grove, Beckett suggested that all Barney's authors should donate an unpublished manuscript to get him started. He would begin by giving Barney his first play, *Eleutheria* ("liberty" in Greek) written in French, in 1947.

Such authorial generosity was not widespread. The only other one of Barney's writers who offered him anything was Marguerite Duras, whose *The Man Sitting in the Corridor* Barney published in 1991.

No sooner had Beckett volunteered *Eleutheria* than he changed his mind. In answer to Barney's June query as to when he would receive the manuscript, Beckett explained: "I had completely forgotten *Eleutheria*. I have now read it again. With loathing. I cannot translate it. Let alone have it published. Another rash promise made with intent to lighten your burden. Now I have added to it. It goes to my heart to break this bad news. But I must. I'll try to write something worth having for you, if only a few pages. I feel unforgivable, so please forgive me. Much love from guilt-ridden Sam." The "something worth having" was *Stirrings Still*, which Barney published in 1988.

Before he died in 1989, Beckett gave him the typescript of *Eleutheria* but not his permission to publish it. For the next several years, Barney did not think about doing anything with this slightly peculiar gift. In 1993, however, he decided that the world ought to have access to the first work of a Nobel Prize–winning writer. He wrote to Jérome Lindon, Beckett's French publisher and literary executor, asking for authority to publish it. The answer, both from Lindon and Edward Beckett, the writer's nephew and representative of his estate, was an unambiguous "no." Their position was straightforward: as Samuel Beckett did not think it worthy of being published or performed, the wishes of the dead author had to be observed. For Lindon and Edward, it was a question of principle, honoring the explicit instructions of the artist. For Barney, it was yet another form of censorship, denying the public the right to experience a distinguished author's work. He argued that the world was the richer for Max Brod's refusal to honor Franz

Kafka's request to destroy his manuscripts. He also pointed out that Beckett had been known to change his mind about what of his was publishable. In 1964, when Grove was readying *More Pricks Than Kicks* for publication, Beckett wrote Barney that having looked at it after a quarter of a century, he had realized that "this old shit" was not redeemable and asked Barney to stop production. In 1970, he permitted Grove to go ahead with it. And after indicating his firm opposition in a 1960 letter to the publication in English of *Mercier et Camier*, he didn't object to its coming out in 1975. So, for Barney, Lindon's claim that even a few days before his death Beckett remained adamant about not letting *Eleutheria* be included among his complete works was not compelling. His rigidities had proved flexible in the past.

Barney continued to skirmish throughout 1993 with Edward and Lindon, who refused to budge. "I consider our discussion about *Eleutheria* as ended," Lindon wrote to Barney in April. Resistance, of course, always served as a goad to Barney, who only became more unrelenting the more ferocious the battle. If Lindon deemed the issue closed, Barney would move ahead on his own. In September 1994, he obtained a translation from Albert Bermel and arranged a production for the New York Theater Workshop. Speaking for the estate, Edward Beckett condemned Barney's behavior as "not only illegal but morally disgraceful," and warned he would bring a suit against any organization participating in the play's production. Under these circumstances, the Theater Workshop demanded a $25,000 bond from Barney if there were to be a performance, something he could not supply. Instead, he collected the audience of one hundred invited guests outside of the (locked) theater and went with the cast to his Fourth Avenue apartment building, which also housed the American Mime Theater. The thirteen actors then conducted a reading of the seventeen roles in the theater, as opposed to giving an actual performance of the play. For his subversive efforts, the Beckett estate, in the person of Edward, dismissed Barney as Beckett's North American theatrical agent.

Barney remained unfazed by the loss of his profitable agent's role and no less determined to act. Having earlier, with two publishing colleagues, John Oakes and Dan Simon, formed Foxrock, a company named after Beckett's birthplace in Ireland, for the express purpose of publishing *Eleutheria*, Barney sent a catalogue to Lindon announcing the play's forthcoming appearance. Lindon immediately threatened legal proceedings against anybody associated with it in any way, as producers, translators, or distributors. Barney then engaged lawyer Martin Garbus, who went to US District Court to seek a declaratory judgment freeing the play to be published. In order to avoid the charge that Barney and his publishing colleagues were interested solely in making a profit on the play, the three decided to publish a limited, not-for-sale edition, and commissioned another translation by Michael Brodsky.

Understanding that Barney's commitment to his cause would not permit him to give up, Lindon finally did. In January of 1995, he wrote to Barney that, although he felt certain that Beckett would not have wanted the play to be made available, "Yet as I see you are staunchly bent on publishing your translation, I bring myself to grant you that publication right for the United States which you have been asking me for." The play was by no means a commercial success as a text, but Barney had at least managed to get it before the public. Barney, in any case, had never shared Lindon's concern that the real loser in having the play published would be Beckett. Lindon's (and Beckett's for that matter) lack of regard for it led him to worry that any reader coming to Beckett for the first time through *Eleutheria* might well be turned off the writer. In the preface to the play's French edition, Lindon expressed this anxiety directly: "ne pas rester là," he cautions the reader, "do not stay there." No evidence exists that Barney's commitment to publish *Eleutheria* cost Beckett any enthusiastic readers.

Barney's ouster from Grove marked the first of three painful terminations of important long-term relationships that occurred in the 1980s. The second was with Joan Mitchell, the wife he had divorced in 1952. The breakup of their marriage had not ended their friendship. They had remained in touch over the years, exchanging loving letters and supporting each other emotionally through difficult times. Barney visited her occasionally at her home in Vétheuil, France, with his different wives and children. She liked his children but was more skeptical of his wives, each of whom, Barney reported, she frequently insulted. In the summer of 1989, Barney's chronic need of money drove him to ask Joan if he could borrow $50,000 from her. Joan angrily refused, accusing him of having spent all his money on call girls. She added that she didn't have any to spare because she owed the French government $1 million in taxes. But if Barney would give her his phone number, she would have her lawyer call him.

On August 2, deeply offended by both the rejection and her nasty tone, Barney wrote to Joan from Reilly's Bar on Third Avenue and 23rd Street, "without," as he says, "call girls, without anybody, just his memories and a rum and coke." He explains to her how much he has loved her and how her cruelty has hurt him. He then instructs her on what an appropriate response would have been:

"Gee Barney, it's awfully tough right now, and I don't think I can do anything for you, but I will try and if there is anything left after paying my bills—you will hear from me. But in the meantime, Buck Up—we all love you. Remember, you accomplished a lot, more than most people, and that means something, etc., etc."

He points out that if she had just loaned him the money instead of snarling at him to sell the five paintings of hers he owned (for the $50,000 he needed, Barney's worst business deal ever), they both would have been better off. But she allowed spite to overcome her rationality.

Barney finishes by lamenting the suffering she inflicted: "My dearest, you made me very sad. Not a nice way to end things." However harshly she turned against him, Barney, who never enjoyed losing, found a way to claim a victory of sorts: "Well, you CAN'T stop me from loving you until I die. So there." An indistinct Barney scrawl of a female figure seemingly on a bicycle, entitled "Portrait of Joan," concludes the letter. Joan didn't answer, and they never spoke again. She died in 1992.

The third failure involved his marriage to Lisa, his fourth wife. The relationship had begun to fall apart during his negotiations with Weidenfeld and Getty. Both spouses knew it was coming to an end. Barney wanted it to continue, but Lisa couldn't endure the emotional abuse at Barney's hands that she understood would never change. The excitement of life with Barney was real, but the alcohol-fueled savaging that went along with it finally proved too much. "It was easy to love Barney," Lisa commented, "it was hard to live with him." They were divorced in 1990.

Barney was out of Grove but by no means out of publishing. In addition to his prolonged but ultimately successful struggle over *Eleutheria*, Barney published several other significant books under the Foxrock imprint, including Beckett's gift to him, *Stirrings Still* (1988), the last piece he wrote; two Oe novels, *Seventeen* and *J* (1991); and Duras's *The Man Sitting in the Corridor* (1991). In 1986, he formed Rosset and Company to publish *Two Dogs and Freedom*, a moving collection of essays, letters, and drawings from the children of Soweto in South Africa. The book explores their aspirations for lives free from the limitations imposed by apartheid. The title comes from one eight-year-old's dream of having a "wife and two children, a boy and a girl, a big house and two dogs and freedom." Precisely the kind of book Barney felt a moral imperative to publish, regardless of its capacity to sell.

But his major activity was in developing the Victorian Library of adult fiction that Weidenfeld had sold him as an incentive to settle with Grove. These were the soft-core paperbacks Barney didn't need Grove's permission to publish. He named the line, which he launched in 1987, Blue Moon Books, as in "Once in a Blue Moon . . . will you find the real thing." Whatever else Barney could do, he certainly knew how to make money out of erotica. With their seductive covers, largely anonymous authorships, and explicitly designated areas of interest—Victorian Era, Legendary Age, Jazz Age, and New Tempo—the better to guide readers to their sexual preferences, the books sold well. By 1989, Blue Moon was coming out with three books a month, and Barney was projecting sales that year of a million dollars. He appeared to have stabilized himself following the Grove fiasco—until, that is, the man who had put an end to censorship in this country was set upon again by the censors. This time it was not postmasters, district attorneys, or indignant feminists but a Methodist minister living in Mississippi, who was intent on keeping America wholesome for the American family. One night in December 1976, the Reverend Donald Wildmon suddenly realized there was no prime-time television show his respectable family with young children could watch. Incensed, he decided to give up his ministry and go out instead to do battle with the forces of pornography and violence in the media, as well as the plague of sleazy advertising infecting the country. A year later, he established the National Federation for Decency, which turned into the more appealing American Family Association (AFA) in 1988. His weapons in defense of traditional Christian values were not litigation or sit-ins but the rather more potent means of commercial boycotts. Burger King and Pepsi Cola had already felt its wrath for unseemly advertisements. In 1990, the AFA discovered the large number of Blue Moon paperbacks listed under "anonymous" authorship that filled the shelves of the big bookstore chains like Waldenbooks and B. Dalton. It provided the perfect opportunity for the AFA to flex its moral muscle. The organization threatened to boycott Kmart, owner of Waldenbooks, if they continued to carry Barney's dirty works. When the "Tupelo Ayatollah" (*Playboy's* name for Wildmon, born in Tupelo, Mississippi) spoke, buyers listened, and in short order Waldenbooks rid itself of its Blue Moon stock. Although the AFA didn't target Barnes & Noble and the B. Dalton chain they owned, they too heard the Ayatollah's warning; in six months, Barnes & Noble and Waldenbooks together slashed Barney's Blue Moon business by 60 percent. Barney asked Barnes & Noble not to tear the cover off (standard procedure when returning mass market paperbacks) but to send back the entire book, at Blue Moon's expense, so that Barney might place the books elsewhere. Barnes & Noble refused. Stripping twenty-five thousand covers off the books they were getting rid of, they ruined approximately 15 percent of his inventory.

Ironically, what finally destroyed Blue Moon books was not Wildmon's calculated commercial assault but a libel suit that had nothing at all to do with Barney. In the summer of 1997, Steve Wynn, Las Vegas casino magnate, brought suit against Barricade Books, which had published an unauthorized biography of him. Wynn's case was not against the volume itself but the Barricade catalogue which, in describing the book's contents, alleged that it reveals why a Scotland Yard report associated Wynn with the Genovese crime family. Wynn charged he was defamed; the jury found for him, and the judge prohibited Barricade's Brooklyn warehouse from sending out any books. Unfortunately, Barricade also served as Blue Moon's distributor, so the order shutting the warehouse down extended to Barney's books as well. Blue Moon sales stopped entirely. Within a year, Barney had to declare bankruptcy. Had he any lingering doubts, the Reverend Wildmon must have indeed been convinced that the Lord works in mysterious ways.

Barney without Grove struggled, but so did Grove without Barney. Weidenfeld and Getty did not manage to turn the company around, as they thought they would, particularly with the infusion of Getty money. Although Getty's resources were basically unlimited, still there were limits, and her financial advisors began to recommend that she cut her losses. In 1990, she consented to put Grove up for sale. As soon as Barney learned that Grove might be available, he cobbled together a group of publishers, several of whom, like Kent Carroll, Herman Graf, and John Oakes, had previously worked for him at Grove, and made an offer of $11.5 million to regain the business. Getty again refused, unwilling to give back to Barney the company she had purchased from him five years earlier. But stubbornness and business acumen are not identical. Rejecting Barney didn't improve Grove's bottom line, nor did a scaled-back production schedule. In 1993, the moment had come for Getty to renounce her publishing fantasies. A merger was announced between the Atlantic Monthly Press, led by Morgan Entrekin, and Grove. The new organization, with Entrekin at the helm, would be known as Grove/Atlantic.

Although Barney's post-Grove publishing commitments kept him busy, they could not restore him to prominence. Together, Rosset and Co., Foxrock, and Blue Moon Books were no substitute for the incandescent business he had crafted from practically nothing in 1951. But even if he had stayed with the company, Barney would not have been able to keep doing what he had managed for nearly three decades. The times that permitted him to flourish had changed; and the Grove he had invented, which shaped American culture the way no other publisher did, had come and gone. The nineties bore little resemblance to the volatile sixties. The radical politics he espoused, which helped to turn the country against the Vietnam war, had faded to sacred memory; the brilliant European avant-garde writers Barney brought to these shores had become academically certified, mainstream figures, no longer exotic and controversial; the sexually titillating could now be found everywhere.

However diminished by his expulsion from Grove, Barney was not inclined to give up or lament. He looked firmly toward the future, refusing to dwell on the mistakes of the past. When Blue Moon went out of business in 1998, Barney started the *Evergreen Review* website. He encouraged open submissions from anyone interested, and read them all personally. The publication of *Two Dogs and Freedom* in 1987 brought him into contact with Astrid Myers, an energetic kindergarten and first grade teacher in South Hampton who shared Barney's political passions—she was chair of the Democratic Party in East Hampton—and wanted some copies of the book for her students. She got both the book and Barney himself. "Romance," Barney noted, followed their initial meeting, and shortly afterwards they moved in together. Barney wanted to marry Astrid early in their relationship, but she could see no point. His celebrated persuasiveness, particularly when it came to enticing women into marriage, took longer than usual this time, but he kept at it and with the encouragement of her friends, Astrid finally became the fifth Mrs. Rosset in 2007.

Life without a steady income was challenging, but Barney found ways to manage. He sold his archives to Columbia; he received a grant from the New York State Council on the Arts; he sold his Joan Mitchell correspondence and photographs he had taken of her to the Joan Mitchell Foundation; he sold his East Hampton house; and he and Astrid rented out her East Hampton house every summer. He resorted to the ancient practice of barter to help with the rent of his Fourth Avenue loft, giving the landlord one painting by Henry Miller and one by Larry Rivers in lieu of cash.

The sale of his archives in 2010 opened the way to a titanic outpouring of creative energy on Barney's part, which occupied him until his death. Having denuded the shelves in his loft of their contents of books and papers, he removed the empty bookcases from the wall, took down paintings that had also been hanging there, and exposed a vast, empty space, twelve feet high and twenty-two feet long. Without offering any reasons, he then began to turn the wall into a mural and collage, and never stopped working on it. According to Astrid, "He had to fill that space. He had to fill that emptiness. He had to feel like change was still occurring." Painting the wall became an obsessively absorbing project with no end. He would paint for hours at a time. When scaling a stepladder to paint near the ceiling became too perilous, he would tape a paint brush to a pool cue or cane to get to the high spots. He continuously revised his revisions, affixed wooden dioramas to the wall, and installed and removed various Styrofoam constructions. Astrid particularly liked the cuff links he glued to an abstract face as its eyes. The dioramas contained obvious autobiographical references—toy soldiers in one to allude to his war experiences in China; skeletons playing pool suggest his own passion for the game in another—but the notion, maintained by some, that the wall should be read as an acrylic autobiography, seems a stretch. Barney never explained what he was doing, never felt he had to explain. The wall permitted him total immersion in a creative universe of his own imagining that delighted and sustained him. What others made of it hardly mattered. Several friends suggested it was the last work Barney ever published.

If, during his Astrid years, Barney didn't have the money his accomplishments should have commanded, he at least had enough for the foreign travel he loved—Paris, China, India, Laos, Cambodia, Vietnam, Nicaragua, Mexico, Stockholm in 1994 for Kenzaburo Oe's Nobel Prize ceremony, and Thailand. He particularly liked Thailand, which he visited on numerous occasions, admiring the beauty of its women as much as the beauty of the country. He even forgave Ann Getty enough for dumping him from Grove to ask, in 1991, if she would be interested in investing in a hotel he wanted to lease in Pattaya. He was prepared to live there and open an art gallery in it. She never answered his letter.

Barney led a somewhat more subdued existence with Astrid than he had previously. He no longer needed to go out for dinner every night, as he did with Lisa, or drink after dinner until the early morning. Both age and budget realities curbed his excesses. There were friends and parties, of course, but he avoided the frenetic pace of the younger Barney, except when it came to tending to the trees of Astrid's property. Despite his urban origins, Barney loved outdoor nature work. He toiled ceaselessly on the grounds of his East Hampton houses over the years, insisting that his children and their friends join him if they came out for weekends. They resented it but had no choice. Weeding and planting were required. He would not permit slackers. When he and Astrid drove out to her home, he would leave the car and go directly to begin laboring on the trees and shrubs, pruning, planting, digging them up, and replanting them. Astrid called him her "tree man."

The person who was once told by the president of Random House that he considered him to be "outside the mainstream of

American publishing" lived long enough to see his courageous efforts to change the world finally appreciated by the publishing establishment. In 1988, he received the PEN American Center Publisher Citation for "distinction and continuous service to international letters, to the freedom and dignity of writers, and to the free transmission of the printed word across the barriers of poverty, ignorance, censorship and repression." The French minister of culture made him a Commandeur de l'Ordre des Arts et Lettres in 1999, declaring that many of the notable books of our age were made available by Grove Press. In 2008, the National Book Foundation gave him a Lifetime Achievement Award, citing his "vision and enormous contribution to American publishing." He was also honored by the Small Press Center, the National Book Critics Circle, the Association of American Publishers, the *Paris Review*, the National Coalition against Censorship, and the Norman Mailer Foundation.

Of all the distinctions he earned, he seems to have valued a little-known one more than the grander public acknowledgments. In February 2012, several days before his death, he and Astrid gave a party in their loft in honor of his daughter Chantal's wedding. Chatting with his cousin, Mary Morris, he pointed to a large volume on the bookshelf and asked her to bring it over to him. Entitled *Whatever Happened to Sex in Scandinavia?*, it was published by the Office for Contemporary Art, a foundation established by the Norwegian government. "Look at this," he said to her, "it's dedicated to me. This is the most important thing ever to happen in my life." Puzzled, Mary wondered how he could make such a claim. The answer, from the "Anti-Everything" high school editor who spent his whole career struggling against the US government and whom it in turn harassed, accused of disloyalty, and tried to undermine, has an unexpected poignancy to it: "Because a government has dedicated a book to me."

In 2002, Barney underwent aortic valve replacement surgery. Pig or cow replacements tend to wear out after ten years. In 2012, Barney learned he was suffering from aortic stenosis, a narrowing of the aorta. He would need another procedure; otherwise, he might have less than a year to live. At his age, obviously not a risk-free undertaking, but Barney was nothing if not a risk taker. Extensive deliberations with his family endorsed his decision to undergo the operation. Accompanied by Astrid and his two sons, Peter and Beckett, he went to Columbia Presbyterian Hospital in New York early in the morning of February 21. The surgery appeared to be successful, though there was some bleeding that the doctors thought they could stop. They were wrong. They advised the family to go home at eight o'clock that night, saying they would inform them of Barney's progress. By nine o'clock, Allen Ginsberg's "publisher-hero," whom the influential New York theater critic Jerry Tallmer called "a Tom Paine of the human brain," had died.

ACKNOWLEDGMENTS

I am grateful to the friends, associates, and relatives of Barney Rosset who shared their memories of this complicated, fascinating man with me. I would like to thank, in alphabetical order, Joe Bianco, Georges Borchardt, Morgan Entrekin, Jason Epstein, Martin Garbus, Herman Graf, Dan Green, Richard Howard, Chantal Rosset Hyde, Fred Jordan, Ken Jordan, Lisa Krug, Claudia Menza, Mary Morris, John Oakes, Astrid Myers Rosset, Ed Sanders, Jeanette Seaver, Ira Silverberg, Nat Sobel, and Haskell Wexler. In particular, I am indebted to Ken and Fred, Lisa, Claudia, Astrid, and Chantal, who not only spoke with me at length but also went out of their way to help me with various odd questions I would put to them. Patricia Albers was especially kind in helping me unravel some of the complications of Barney's relationship with Joan Mitchell. The Rosset papers in Columba University's Rare Book and Manuscript Library in Butler Library were an invaluable source of insight and information about Barney and Grove Press, and the reference librarians always made sure research time there was profitably spent. Both individually and corporately, they were wonderfully helpful. I listened to the audio tapes that Loren Glass deposited at the Syracuse University Special Collections Research Center. My thanks also to my research assistant Michael Abolafia, who tracked down elusive references for me.

This book never would have happened if it had not been for the loving friendship, encouragement, and wisdom of Nick Lyons, who was there at the very beginning and saw the project through to the end. His support was critical; every page benefitted from his having read it. I was also fortunate to have access to Cal Barksdale's keen eye and editorial savvy, on both of which I came to depend.

The other indispensable presence was that of my wife, Judith, whose small check marks she delicately placed in the margins of the manuscript always had large consequences. We both know the extent to which *Barney* was in every sense a collaborative enterprise.

NOTES

With the exceptions noted below, all the quoted material in the text comes from the Barney Rosset Papers, deposited in Columbia University's Rare Book and Manuscript Library located in Butler Library.

Introduction
7 purely personal: Herman Graf, conversation with author.

8 one of us has to go: Claudia Menza, conversation with author.

8 We're having too much fun here.: Richard Seaver, *The Tender Hour of Twilight* (New York: Farrar, Straus and Giroux, 2012), 366.

9 Posterity repeatedly: *The Review of Contemporary Fiction: Grove Press Number*, vol 10, no. 3 (Fall 1990), 142.

2 Joan and Barney
45 Let's be bourgeois pigs.: Patricia Albers, *Joan Mitchell, Lady Painter: A Life* (New York: Alfred A. Knopf, 2011), 133.

48 She had a: John Ashbery, *Joan Mitchell* catalogue (New York: Robert Miller Gallery, 1992).

48 in the deep sense: Albers, *Joan Mitchell, Lady Painter*, 136.

3 The Young Publisher
53 function was: John Gruen, *The Party's Over* (New York: Viking Press, 1972), 41.

54 Thus began: Gruen, *The Party's Over*, 42.

5 The Stalking Horse
100 The contemporary community: Charles Rembar, *The End of Obscenity* (New York: Harper & Row, 1968), 117.

102 that the reason: Edward de Grazia, *Girls Lean Back Everywhere* (New York: Vintage Books, 1993), 320.

103 book is almost: Rembar, *The End of Obscenity*, 142.

104 The decision of: Rembar, *The End of Obscenity*, 382.

104 It is essential: Rembar, *The End of Obscenity*, 344.

6 Adventures with the Hooded Cobra
109 the dignity of: Earl R. Hutchinson, *Tropic of Cancer on Trial* (New York: Grove Press, 1968), 4.

111 What I have: Jay Martin, *Always Merry and Bright: The Life of Henry Miller* (California: Capra Press, 1978), 462.

115 the method of: Elmer Gertz, *A Handful of Clients* (Chicago: Follett Publishing Company, 1965), 265.

116 I would imagine: Gertz, *A Handful of Clients*, 271.

128 Americans were finally: Ted Morgan, *Literary Outlaw: The Life and Times of William Burroughs* (New York: Avon Books, 1988) 347.

7 Riding the Gales of the Sixties
130 1001 ways to beat the draft: Tuli Kupferberg and Robert Bashlow, *1001 Ways to Beat the Draft* (New York: Grove Press, 1967).

134 A harsh introduction: Seaver, *The Tender Hour of Twilight*, 369.

136 was wildly excited: John Nathan, *Living Carelessly in Tokyo and Elsewhere* (New York: Free Press, 2008), 116.

136 John Nathan's cowardly: Nathan, *Living Carelessly*, 117.